THE
GOSPEL
FOR LIFE

—— SERIES ——

THE GOSPEL &

Pornography

Also in the *Gospel for Life* series

THE
GOSPEL
FOR LIFE

—— SERIES ——

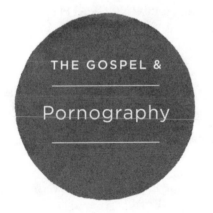

THE GOSPEL &

Pornography

SERIES EDITORS

RUSSELL MOORE *and*
ANDREW T. WALKER

B&H
PUBLISHING GROUP

NASHVILLE, TENNESSEE

978-1-4336-9045-7

Published by B&H Publishing Group
Nashville, Tennessee

Dewey Decimal Classification: 363.4
Subject Heading: PORNOGRAPHY \ BIBLE. N.T.
GOSPELS \ EROTICA

1 2 3 4 5 6 7 8 • 21 20 19 18 17

CONTENTS

- *Objectification and Porn*
- *The Peopling of the World*

Series Preface

Russell Moore

Why Should the *Gospel for Life* Series Matter to Churches?

IN ACTS CHAPTER 2, WE READ ABOUT THE DAY OF PENTECOST, the day when the resurrected Lord Jesus sent the Holy Spirit from heaven onto His church. The Day of Pentecost was a spectacular day—there were manifestations of fire, languages being spoken by people who didn't know them, and thousands of unbelievers coming to faith in this recently resurrected Messiah. Reading this passage, we go from account to account of heavenly shock and awe, and yet the passage ends in an unexpectedly simple way: "And they devoted themselves to the apostles' teaching and the fellowship, to the breaking of bread, and the prayers" (Acts 2:42 ESV).

I believe one thing the Holy Spirit wants us to understand from this is that these "ordinary" things are not less spectacular than what preceded them—in fact, they may be more so. The disciplines of discipleship, fellowship, community, and prayer are the signs that tell us the kingdom of Christ is here. That means that for Christians, the most crucial moments in our walk with Jesus Christ don't happen in the thrill of "spiritual highs." They happen in the common hum of everyday life in quiet, faithful obedience to Christ.

That's what the *Gospel for Life* series is about: taking the truths of Scripture, the story of our redemption and adoption by a risen Lord Jesus, and applying them to the questions and situations that we all face in the ordinary course of life.

Our hope is that churches will not merely find these books interesting, but also helpful. The *Gospel for Life* series is meant to assist pastors and church leaders to answer urgent questions that people are asking, questions that the church isn't always immediately ready to answer. Whether in a counseling session or alongside a sermon series, these books are intended to come alongside church leaders in discipling members to see their lives with a Kingdom mentality.

Believers don't live the Christian life in isolation but rather as part of a gospel community, the church. That's why we have structured the *Gospel for Life* series to be easily utilized in anything from a small group study context to a new member or new believer class. None of us can live worthy of the gospel by ourselves, and thankfully, none have to.

Why are we so preoccupied with the idea of living life by and through the gospel? The answer is actually quite simple: because the gospel changes everything. The gospel isn't a mere theological system or a political idea, though it shapes both our theology and our politics. The gospel is the Good News that there is a Kingdom far above and beyond the borders of this world, where death is dead and sin and sorrow cease. The gospel is about how God brings this Kingdom to us by reconciling us to Himself through Christ.

That means two things. First, it means the gospel fulfills the hopes that our idols have promised and betrayed. The Scripture says that all God's promises are yes in Jesus (2 Cor. 1:20). As sinful human beings, we all tend to think what we really want is freedom from authority, inheritance without obedience like the prodigal son. But what Jesus offers is the authority we were designed to live under, an inheritance we by no means deserve to share, and the freedom that truly satisfies our souls.

Second, this means that the gospel isn't just the start of the Christian life but rather the vehicle that carries it along. The gospel is about the daily reality of living as an adopted child of a resurrected Father-King, whose Kingdom is here and is still coming. By looking at our jobs, our marriages, our families, our government, and the entire universe through a gospel lens, we live differently. We will work and marry and vote with a Kingdom mind-set, one that prioritizes the permanent things of

Christ above the fleeting pleasures of sin and the vaporous things of this world.

The *Gospel for Life* series is about helping Christians and churches navigate life in the Kingdom while we wait for the return of its King and its ultimate consummation. The stakes are high. To get the gospel wrong when it comes to marriage can lead to a generation's worth of confusion about what marriage even is. To get the gospel wrong on adoption can leave millions of "unwanted" children at the mercy of ruthless sex traffickers and callous abusers. There's no safe space in the universe where getting the gospel wrong will be merely an academic blunder. That's why these books exist—to help you and your church understand what the gospel is and what it means for life.

Theology doesn't just think; it walks, weeps, and bleeds. The *Gospel for Life* series is a resource intended to help Christians see their theology do just that. When you see all of life from the perspective of the Kingdom, everything changes. It's not just about miraculous moments or intense religious experiences. Our gospel is indeed miraculous, but as the disciples in Acts learned, it's also a gospel of the ordinary.

Introduction

Andrew T. Walker

THE MOST DANGEROUS SINS TO OUR CHRISTIAN LIFE ARE THE ones we think are anonymous.

That sentence might strike you as a little unclear or even mysterious. An accidental swear word coming out of your mouth in reaction to stubbing your toe might be embarrassing, but for anyone within earshot of hearing it, they'll likely shrug it off. No less in need of repenting than other sins, these sins aren't the ones we most desire to hide. They weren't really deliberate; they were thoughtless and careless.

But certain sins require anonymity. They require an intentionality to them that aren't required of other sins. Enter pornography—perhaps the most widespread, supposedly anonymous sin afflicting both American culture and the culture of the local church.

The man or woman trapped in an unending cycle of guilt and despair over pornography addiction thinks their sin is anonymous. They can erase the history on their browser. They can

1

believe that the sermon at church that mentions pornography is about someone else's problem.

And that's exactly what the Devil wants. The Devil wants to delude and confuse each of us into thinking that our sins are only our problem; that they can be hidden away in our memory and not come back to inflict our conscience with cutting reminders of guilt. The Devil wants each of us to believe that we can rid ourselves of guilt and shame apart from Jesus. That's what the Devil is always up to—offering both the sin that rejects Christ, but also rescue plans that bypass Christ. As Christians, we have to reject both of these patterns. We have to focus on Jesus, who can rewire darkened hearts.

Pornography seems to be everywhere in today's culture, and even worse, is laughed off as something routine, instead of a commercialized industry preying on people's marriages and purity. Porn is a "public health crises" according to some social commentary, but it's more than just that. Pornography is a driving factor in America's marriage crisis and abuse crisis. To love our culture, we're going to have to be honest about porn's effect on our society. If Christians are going to fight the unending sexualizing of American culture, we're going to have to address the problem in our own midst, for the integrity of the Christian witness on sexuality requires an intentional pursuit of purity.

That's why we chose pornography to be in the *Gospel for Life* series. It's an issue that can't be ignored. And while there are excellent resources available on combating and healing from pornography, we were convinced that the sheer abundance of pornography in today's culture required us to address it here as well.

Each book in the *Gospel for Life* series is structured the same: What are we for? What does the gospel say? How should the Christian live? How should the church engage? What does the culture say?

The Gospel & Pornography is intended to be an introductory look at the issue of pornography from every angle of the Christian's life—their place in culture, their engagement as everyday Christians, and their role in the body of Christ, the church. We want no stone unturned when talking about how the gospel of Jesus Christ shapes us as a people on mission for God in every sphere of our life—specifically with an issue that threatens the witness, purity, and spiritual vitality of so many Christians.

We hope that as you come away from this volume, you'll have a better understanding of the underlining theological, cultural, and social issues involved, and will be better equipped to reject the counter-gospel message offered by the pornography industry. We hope that you will experience victory rooted in the freeing message of the gospel in an area of deep brokenness and sin.

We hope you'll see from the Bible that God is not squeamish or uncomfortable when it comes to addressing issues of sexuality and pornography, because He cares about the holistic well-being of His children. In our technological age, pornography is dangerous, pervasive, and accessible. But the Christian worldview presents a vision of hope and a model for victory. To this we now turn.

CHAPTER

1

What Are We For?

Trevin Wax

"THOU SHALT NOT LOOK AT PORN."

If you dig into the Bible looking for a clear-cut prohibition of pornography, you'll come up empty. That doesn't mean God is okay with it, of course. A wise reader of Scripture sets the practice of viewing pornography next to multiple biblical principles, and it is those principles that lead us to the conclusion that God stands against this behavior.

Pornography is a vice that touches on many aspects of human sinfulness: the glorification of sex outside of marriage, the objectification of other human beings made in God's image, the fanning of the flames of lust, and the indulgence of our worst instincts. Because of these aspects of human sin, most people have an undefined, yet accurate understanding that the Bible condemns pornographic imagery. It's why we speak of pornography as something dangerous, something to avoid, an addictive indulgence that warps and distorts our sexuality.

"Keep Away" Is Not Enough

The response of the church is simple: "Keep away!" Discussions about pornography often resemble the skull and crossbones you see on bottles of poison, a warning about the damage that can be done by whatever is inside. *Death is in this bottle,* says the label.

I resonate with the starkness of this kind of warning. Like almost all men today (and an increasing number of women), I've seen pornography, felt the power of its allure, and have witnessed its devastating consequences. I've seen marriages dissolve under the weight of betrayal and distrust. I've walked alongside others who have asked for support in their struggle to overcome pornographic addiction. I've signed up myself, and others, for Internet filters and accountability programs.

But what if we're missing an opportunity here? What if, in our "no" to pornography, we're missing the chance to show what the Bible says "yes" to? What if our attention gets so focused on avoiding sexual sin that we fail to see the beauty of sexuality, as defined by our Creator?

I don't recommend we soften our "no" to pornography in the least. The response to youthful temptation is to flee, just as the apostle Paul commanded and the Old Testament character Joseph demonstrated. There are times when you don't fight or try to stay afloat, when temptation is not to be trifled with. You change the situation. You flee the place where temptation is hounding you. Pornography is that kind of temptation.

But alongside our "no" to pornography must come the Bible's "yes" to sexual expression within the marital union. The Bible doesn't start with "no." The Bible doesn't explicitly address pornography at all. Instead, God's Word gives us a bigger story, and within that overarching story line, the use of pornography becomes something unthinkable.

No one who takes the Bible seriously will arrive at the conclusion that pornography is acceptable for Christians—something to shrug your shoulders at, as if it is something to be expected as boys come of age. No. "Boys will be boys" is not a phrase found in Scripture. The biblical command is to "act like men" and "flee youthful lusts." The world sees porn as something to be managed; the Bible sees it as something to be killed.

Pornography within the Story of God's Good World

The purpose of this opening chapter is to dig a little deeper into the story of God's good world. Here we find a drama that unfolds from the first book of the Bible until the last. A glorious marriage between a man and woman opens the Bible's story of humanity, and a glorious marriage of heaven and earth, and of Jesus and His bride brings about the closing of this age and the beginning of God's never-ending sequel.

Within the context of this story, we come to understand why pornography makes no sense when compared to God's good design. But we also discover the reasons why pornography maintains such a powerful pull on people today.

So, moving forward, we will start by looking at God's design as set out at the creation of this world. Then, we will look at how humanity has fallen into sin, and how this sinfulness results in the distortion of beauty, sexuality, and human relationships. Finally, we will see the radical response to sexual sin that signifies the presence of God's redemption in our lives. All this will prepare the way for the writers of the next chapters to dig deeper into how we can respond with the power of the gospel to the powerful allure of pornography.

Scan the dial on your radio or browse the music video channels on YouTube and you'll hear song after song after song extolling the beauty of love. Pop songs, rock songs, country songs, and jazz—no matter the genre, we call them "love songs" for a reason. The romantic spark between a man and a woman ignites all the senses and stirs up the deepest emotions in us.

"Love songs" run the gamut of emotion. There are songs of puppy love, songs that express one's initial desire, songs of rugged commitment, songs of exclusive devotion. Then, there are the "break-up songs"—lyrics about feeling alone, protests toward a cheating partner, laments of heartache and divorce, songs that long for reconciliation.

Love songs are everywhere, and as Christians, we shouldn't be surprised. After all, the first recorded words of the first human being, Adam, were a love song.

When God saw that it was not good for Adam to be alone (Gen. 2:18), He made Eve as his helper and complement. And when Adam saw his match for the first time, he burst into song: "This one, at last, is bone of my bone and flesh of my flesh; this one will be called 'woman,' for she was taken from man" (Gen. 2:23). Adam was delighted with the woman God had made. One can almost hear Etta James's voice filling the airwaves of the sky: "At last! My love has come along!"

Genesis 2:23 gives us the forerunner to all the other love songs of the world. You know the type—the never-ending supply of songs that focus on how suitable the lover is for the singer.

"You were meant for me," sang Jewel, "and I was meant for you." There's rich, biblical theology below all this singing about love.

Love and Marriage

Many of the world's love songs go right from romance to sex (or in other, even more problematic cases, from sex to eventual romance). But the first love song recorded in the Bible is different. The biblical text moves from Adam's burst of melodic delight into the truth about marriage: "This is why a man leaves his father and mother and bonds with his wife, and they become one flesh" (Gen. 2:24).

Here is a relationship that includes sexuality, yes, but this union extends to all aspects of the couple's identity. The sexual partnership is the act that unites their bodies, but also intends to express and reestablish the covenant commitment that brings together the spiritual and emotional aspects of a man and woman into harmony. What's his is hers; what's hers is his. Out of the family of father, mother, and child, comes another family.

And so, Adam's delight at seeing his perfect complement is reenacted every time a man sees the first glimpse of his bride walking down the aisle and knows deep down inside, "This is perfect." All of those love songs that express in one way or another the truth that "we were made for each other" are mere signposts pointing toward the cosmic reality of marriage, where the two halves of humanity are joined together in glorious and mysterious bliss.

Naked and Unashamed

Genesis 2 ends on an interesting note. "Both the man and his wife were naked, yet felt no shame" (Gen. 2:25). In the garden of Eden, no clothes were necessary. There was nothing to hide, nothing to be embarrassed about. Because there was no sin, there was no vulnerability, and no awkwardness. The first husband and wife lived together in the garden, at peace with each other, and in the light of their Creator, without even a hint of shame and embarrassment. They were blissful in their love and devotion, perfect in their union.

Naked and unashamed. It's important that we pause here for a moment and realize that the naked human body is not, in and of itself, a bad thing. Because we live in a fallen world where our lusts are easily aroused and our tendency to objectify others is so strong, it is easy for Christians to begin to think of nakedness as inherently evil. This overreaction can lead to theological problems, such as thinking of the human body itself as something sinful or bad.

Some of the earliest Christians struggled with their views of the body and of sexuality. The challenges to Christianity they encountered—from the Gnostics, in particular—denied the goodness of the body and led some believers to think that abstaining from marriage and sex was a higher and more noble calling than the more ordinary task of bearing fruit and having children.

We see no such hesitation in Genesis 2. Here, God gives Adam and Eve to one another, places them in a delightful garden, and fills their calendar with great and noble tasks—the first of which was to be fruitful and multiply, and thus fill the earth with more image-bearers of God. Adam and Eve were to come together, and in the overflow of their love for one another, bring forth new life. *There was no shame because there was no sin.*

In the garden, we see the first humans in perfect relationship with one another and with God. They loved and trusted each other, and they loved and trusted God. The text tells us they walked and talked with God in the cool of the day. No wonder Jesus would later say, "Blessed are the pure in heart, for they will see God" (Matt. 5:8). In the garden, there was no sin to cloud Adam and Eve's vision of God, and no shame to cause them to hide their bodies from each other.

Pure in heart. Naked and unashamed. Fruitful bliss. This is God's original design for humanity, a world where the peace of God flourishes and extends into new life and new tasks, and where sexuality finds its proper place in the unashamed love of a man and his wife.

Forbidden Delight and Desire

Adam saw his naked wife and was delighted. But the next time we see something described as "delightful," and the next time we see a human desiring something, is when the serpent enters the garden to tempt Eve to eat from the forbidden tree. "The woman saw that the tree was good for food and delightful to look at, and that it was desirable for obtaining wisdom" (Gen. 3:6).

First, Eve *saw* that it was good. Nothing in the text indicates that she was wrong. It was a tree that God made. Of course, it was good. Even though it was forbidden to her, still the fruit was good. But notice that this good fruit was on the wrong tree. God had given the first humans the freedom to eat from any tree in the garden, except for this one.

Second, the text says that the fruit was "delightful to look at." And, not surprisingly, this delight to the eyes is what made it "desirable" to Eve. She saw the fruit as good, even though it was forbidden, and then she delighted in looking at it and desired it with all her heart. When Adam and Eve ate from that forbidden fruit, they were taking something good that God had made and directly violating His command. They were grasping for something "delightful" and "desirable" apart from God's original intention and design.

Interesting

Out of Place, Out of Bounds

Here is where the story line of the Bible begins to shed light on our understanding of pornography today. The image of a naked man or a naked woman is not something "bad" or "sinful" in and of itself. It is when that image is designed to entice you to desire something out of its proper place, something out of bounds—that's when pornography exerts its pull on your heart.

Just as Adam and Eve reached out for the fruit on a forbidden tree, the man or woman viewing pornography is grasping for beauty—in this case, the beauty of a man or woman—apart from the one-flesh union where a man and woman are supposed to unite. It is a search for beauty and pleasure in the forbidden forest of lust.

And just as the fruit from the forbidden tree led to knowledge of good and evil and the unrelenting pressure of shame, so also does pornography lead to distorted views of sexuality and the desire to hide. Pornography is the fruit that poisons the mind with parodies and caricatures of God's true design for sex within marriage. The beautiful union of a man and woman, united by their covenant love, is smeared with mud.

Just as Eve sinned after her eyes led her astray, so also does "the lust of the eyes" garner attention in other parts of the Bible. The well-known accountability software, Covenant Eyes, comes from Job's comment about making a covenant with his eyes not to look lustfully at a young virgin. When King David, the warrior who was a man after God's own heart and the greatest king of Israel, saw the beautiful Bathsheba bathing on her roof, he was drawn to her and sent for her. It began with the appetite of his eyes. When Jesus spoke of lust, He mentioned how important it is not to let your eye lead you astray.

The Severing of Sex

Pornography is just one example of sexuality being severed from its original purpose. Even though the Bible doesn't explicitly mention pornography, it gives us a word from which our word *porn* is derived. The Greek word *porneia* encompassed a wide variety of sexual sins outside of marriage—from fornication to adultery to homosexuality. The word often comes up in lists of sins; it's a catchall word that refers to multiple kinds of sexual disobedience. And like all sins, *porneia* separates us from God and the people around us.

In *Divine Sex,* New Zealand pastor Jonathan Grant shows how our society rips sexuality from its proper place and step-by-step severs it from other people. We separate sex from procreation, then separate sex from marriage, and even separate sex from partnership (think of the "recreational" or "casual" sex). Pornography goes further than these other steps, leading to the separation of sex from another person. "As the reasoning goes,"

Grant writes, "why include other people if sex is purely about self-gratification? The rise of online pornography is a natural result of this cultural reasoning."[1]

Just as the sin of Adam and Eve separated them from God and introduced barriers between them in their own relationship, pornography also leads us into the dark shadows of shame and slowly isolates us from the people around us. If sex is a good gift from God designed to bring us joy and bring Him glory, then it's no wonder Satan wants to distort that gift so that we only experience shame and loneliness. In pornography, the "one-flesh union" of a man and a woman becomes the "no-flesh" aloneness of a man or woman before the flickering images of a screen, or in the pages of a novel.

When Adam and Even succumbed to temptation, they immediately ran and hid. They were ashamed. Naked and unashamed at the end of Genesis 2. Naked and ashamed (and hiding) by the middle of Genesis 3.

If you want evidence to show that we instinctively know that pornography is wrong, just consider the fact that we try so hard to hide it. Even unbelievers know how to clear their search bar or delete their cache. No matter how bold and brash the actors may be in a pornographic video, the viewer is usually timid and ashamed, hiding the magazine somewhere in the house, or ready to turn off the phone or computer if anyone were to show up.

The emphasis to hide is one of the strongest urges in the person caught in the lair of pornography. Frustrated by the lonely addiction, the person who watches porn often feels they cannot speak to anyone about this sin. They feel a sense of embarrassment not only because of their behavior but also because of what it says about their ability to control their urges. Running and hiding is the common response to many sins, but the sense of hopelessness and frustration is particularly strong when it comes to pornography. Combined with the loneliness fostered by the private shame of pornography, these emotions take a considerable toll on men and women caught in the cycle of addiction.

The Reduction of Sex

So what happens next? What are the results of this sin and our distortion of beauty? In the first instance, pornography trains the mind to focus primarily on the physical actions of people in various sexual situations. The focus is on the physical.

Don't get me wrong, there is a beautiful, good, and irreducible *physical* dimension to the one-flesh union of a man and a woman—right in line with God's good design. Pornography, however, rips the physical aspect of that one-flesh union out of its covenantal home and substitutes images of men and women involved in physical actions, for the viewing pleasure of someone who (usually) is all by themselves. Pornography reduces sexuality to what is happening with human bodies. It is focused only on the physical. The mystery of the one-flesh union is done away with, and the spiritual dimension of sexual union is ignored altogether. Sex is reduced to bodies in motion.

Once you understand how pornography distorts sexuality by reducing it to the physical, you see why our culture occupies this strange place of wanting to say "sex is everything!" and, at the same time, "sex is nothing."

On the one hand, people say "sex is everything" when they make it seem like one's sexual attractions are the defining aspect of one's identity. Freedom is increasingly seen in terms of having the sexual partner or lifestyle one wants, and having those sexual behaviors affirmed.

On the other hand, people say "sex is nothing" when they shrug their shoulders at sexual activity outside of marriage, or say, "sex is no big deal" or say any consenting sexual activity is "just fun," something recreational, something that doesn't even need a commitment behind it. It's just something fun that consenting adults can do together. That's why pornography is in the "no big deal" category for many in the world. But the Bible does not say, "sex is everything;" nor does it say "sex is nothing." To the first group, the Bible says, "sex is not as important as you think." One does not need a sexual relationship in order to be a full and flourishing human being. Just look at Jesus. Or the dozens of leaders throughout church history who never married, people like last century's global evangelical leader, John Stott, or the German pastor martyred at the hands of the Nazis, Dietrich Bonhoeffer.

To the second group, the Bible says, "sex is a lot more important than you think." Pornography *is* a big deal because it severs sexuality from its proper place, isolates you as a person, and cultivates in you a distorted vision of beauty and morality.

The Distortion of Sex

Another result of pornography is that it creates and inflames an appetite for aberrant sexual practices. A friend of mine once struggled with addiction to pornography. He has been open about how this sin affected his marriage—the unrealistic expectations he had for himself and his wife. It's not just Christians who see that pornography stirs up appetites that are damaging to relationships. The R-rated film *Don Jon,* starring Joseph Gordon Levitt, poses questions about how pornography stilts one's emotional and relational capacity.

C. S. Lewis, in *Mere Christianity,* remarked on our society's crazy focus on sexuality. Imagine, he said, if we were to go into a club where slowly but surely the curtain would come up on a plate full of delicious meat, and the audience were to whoop and holler and yell for more. You'd say that something had gone wrong with the appetites of the people in that crowd. But the curtain comes up on strippers and showgirls or male dancers, and somehow, this reaction is described as totally normal.

Pornography distorts one's view of sex and it leads to further distortions. Talk to someone who has viewed a lot of pornography, and they'll tell you that their tastes and appetites changed over time. What they might have been disgusted at initially eventually became a draw, like developing a taste for poison. To the person caught in pornography's trap, there is often a sense that their addiction is worsening, and yet that acknowledgment is heightened by a sense of hopelessness in breaking the cycle.

The Deadening Effects of Sin

Another result of pornography is, like with all sin, a deadening of the senses and the searing of the conscience. What once was sexually stirring no longer holds any power. That's not because the person watching porn has become more alive, but because they've become more dead.

G. K. Chesterton warned about a society where young people believed it was a badge of honor to consider and engage in things their grandparents never would have entertained. If the grandchildren "get used" to something that their grandparents would have abhorred, it's assumed that the grandchildren are more alive, more courageous, more exciting than their grandparents. But, Chesterton claims, this gets it backwards. "Do not be proud of the fact that your grandmother was shocked at something which you are accustomed to seeing and hearing without being shocked," he writes. "It may mean that your grandmother was an extremely lively and vital [person], and that you are a paralytic. . . . To lose the sense of repugnance from one thing, or regard for another, is exactly so far as it goes to relapse into the vegetation or to return to the dust."[2]

In other words, don't take pride in your dullness. Pornography dulls the senses and closes the mind. It rewires the brain and leads to deleterious effects. And, of course, the deadened mind has a harder and harder time with living relationships. The shortcut of temporary sexual pleasure bypasses the hard work and lasting fruitfulness of truly loving one's spouse.

The Redemptive Radical Response

When the Bible talks about lust, it sounds radical. And in the Scriptures, no one sounds more radical than Jesus. "If your eye causes you to sin, tear it out and throw it away," He says. "For it's better to enter life maimed than to be cast into hell" (Matt. 18:9). Those are some serious stakes. The lust that is stirred up by pornography is not to be toyed with.

For some reason, when many people think of the Bible, they conclude that the Old Testament is full of prohibitions and irrelevant laws, and the New Testament gives us a Jesus who is soft on sin and all-inclusive. They ought to read the Gospels. Jesus is radical when it comes to marriage and sexuality. As Scot McKnight describes Him, "Jesus is a moral zealot."[3] Jesus takes the warnings against sexual sin we find in the book of Proverbs, and He ramps them up. He goes beyond the prohibition of adultery and condemns even the thought. Jesus is going for the heart.

Jesus' zealousness regarding purity is not because He hates us or wants to suppress whatever might be "fun." His zealousness stems from His being radically *for* us. He knows what we were made for. That's why, in His description of marriage, He bypasses Moses' concessions about divorce and hardness of heart and goes straight back to Genesis 1–2. He has the image of Adam and Eve in the back of His mind—their delight in the garden—and He teaches that sexuality must be fulfilled only in the way God originally intended.

Whenever a husband and wife enjoy one another within the union of their covenant love, they are reenacting their marriage vows and reestablishing their exclusive love and devotion for one another. They are tasting just a little bit of that delight in Eden, where they can lie naked and unashamed, fully devoted to one another in heart and mind and body.

Pornography is like a serpent that slithers onto the marriage bed, casting fear and self-doubt in the mind of a husband or wife. Porn is a poisonous partner that spews lies and hatred and lust—whatever it takes to pollute and defile the marriage bed.

Jesus' radical measures against lust are not anti-pornography, but pro-marriage.

He wants to protect and uphold the beauty of God's design for husband and wife at all costs. He never wants His followers to feel trapped in the frustrating cycle of addiction to pornography, where despair and hopelessness compound the loneliness of our sin of lust.

Beholding More Beauty

As important as Jesus' extreme instructions about lust may be, they cannot and should not be taken out of the context of the Bible's big story line. You can gouge out your eyes and still be enslaved to lust. (Literally. That's why there are pornographic magazines in Braille.) You can cut off your arm and still be led astray.

No, the ultimate answer to pornography is not by putting filters on our computers, as helpful as they may be, but in having the changed heart where we see pornography the way God does—as the ridiculous and dangerous substitute it truly is. And *that* only happens when our delight is in something bigger, when our grasping for beauty is not out of place but directed to the right object.

Not even a husband or wife can fully satisfy the human heart's desire for beauty. Only in seeing the beauty of God as He has revealed Himself in Jesus Christ can we be truly set free from the addictive urges of pornographic use. We don't need Jesus to come along and tell us pornography is bad; we need Jesus to come along and set us free—to empower us by His Spirit to resist the sinful urges that once commanded us.

In the end, our minds must be captured by a beauty much bigger than the warped and distorted images of nakedness that flit across our screens. It's only through the beauty of Jesus that our frequent failings can be forgiven, and our enslaved minds can be set free. The Bible doesn't say that the Christian will never struggle with lust or selfishness, but it does promise the day we will be like Jesus—beholding the One in whose image we've been remade. *That* is the hope that we look forward to, the restoration of all things, and the true satisfaction and fulfillment that comes from Living Water, not the polluted wells of this world.

Discussion Questions

1. Why is it important that we treat the Bible as our ultimate authority on sexuality and pornography?
2. In what ways have your church, your small group, or your friends dealt with issues related to pornography in the past? What was it about this approach that was helpful? What was harmful?

3. Why do you think it is important to promote and emphasize God's original design for sexuality, not just God's "no" to pornography use?

4. What are some ways you can continually remind yourself and others about God's good design for sexuality?

What Does the Gospel Say?

Russell Moore

NOVELIST FREDERICK BUECHNER ONCE REFLECTED ON WHAT it was like, as a New Yorker, to walk past the then-prevalent X-rated movie theaters of West 42nd Street in Manhattan, and how scared he was by it all. He was not simply scared by the ugliness of it, he wrote, but by how vulnerable he was to such ugliness. He was simultaneously drawn and repulsed by the pornography, and he wondered why.

He wrote:

What scared the daylights out of me was to see suddenly how drawn we all are, I think, to the very things that appall us—to see how beneath our civilizedness, our religiousness, our humanness, there is that in all of us which remains uncivilized, religionless, subhuman, and which hungers for precisely what Forty-Second Street offers, which is basically the license to be subhuman not just sexually but any other way that appeals to us—the license to use and exploit and devour each other like savages, to devour and destroy our own sweet selves.[4]

Buechner's words here resonated with me when I first read them because I remember, as a young child, walking past Bourbon Street in New Orleans, with my grandparents on our way through the French Quarter. My grandparents would walk faster as they held my hand and tried to distract my attention, but the strip clubs were all there, sometimes with carnival-barker types on the sidewalk beckoning people to come in.

Like Buechner, I found the experience somewhat scary. What went on in those places, I wondered, and why do people go there? But they stayed in my memory in a way the other businesses did not.

This paradox of pornography, of a simultaneous allure and repulsion, was even more clear to see when I started, as a pastor, counseling with those caught up in it. Some of them had been immersed in pornography since they were ten or eleven years old. Some happened upon it during some stressful and spiritually dry time in mid-life. These people, usually men, had a certain sort of common self-loathing about them.

Maybe that's where you are, as you read this. You feel disgusted by this, and yet you feel the draw toward it, persistently. And, if you are someone who wants to follow Jesus, there's probably also a good deal of fear mixed in with your shame. Are you on your way to a place so dark that you cannot find your way out? Here, as with all things, the gospel is foundational. Jesus announced, from the very beginning of His ministry, that He was here "to proclaim release to the captives" (Luke 4:18). That includes those who are in captivity or on their way to captivity or fear they may be drawn into captivity to pornography.

The first step toward grappling with this problem is recognizing what's behind it. The apostle John has told us, "For everything in the world—the lust of the flesh, the lust of the eyes, and the pride in one's possessions—is not from the Father, but is from the world" (1 John 2:16). Over the years, Christians have often summarized the sources of our temptations as "the world, the flesh, and the Devil," which is a good synthesis of how the Bible speaks of it. If you're tempted toward pornography, all three of these are working together in your life.

First, there is the world. Since humanity's pre-historic Fall, we have wandered in exile, from that lost place where heaven and earth were joined together, a place the Bible calls Eden. We are sentenced to death, and cut off from the Tree of Life, in a cosmos that now is under the reign of death and the tyranny of powers opposed to God (Gen. 3:24). Contrary to those who peddle the myth of some golden age in the recent past followed by sudden cultural decline, the world has always been a pornographic place. Look as far back as the graffiti of ancient civilizations or the fertility idols of the earliest tribes of humanity.

That's not to say, though, that the temptation to pornography is the same in every age. Some things have indeed changed, in ways that now make the pull toward pornography nearly ubiquitous in Western culture, even within the pews of the church. In a previous generation, there were many stops short of the Holy Spirit restraining people from a full immersion in pornography. Teenagers would pass around a copy of someone's father's *Playboy* magazine or find a way to unscramble the naked channel on someone's satellite dish. But in order to walk into one of those strip clubs or peep shows in New York or New Orleans, or to walk into one of those roadside movie theaters, one had to make certain decisions ahead of time about how one would view oneself. Once you went behind that curtain in the video rental store or walked up to that cashier with that magazine, you had decided that you were willing to be the kind of person who was willing to be thought of, if only by this stranger (but more important to yourself), as the kind of person who would do this.

To be sure, many people did—at first with hearts pounding and sweaty palms and then, of course, it became easier and easier. But the predictable shame of it all limited the pool of those who would be drawn in.

Most of us want to sin while still thinking of ourselves as good people. When I get sinfully angry, I like to tell myself it's "spiritual indignation." When I'm prayerlessly anxious, I like to tell myself that I'm just "planning out all the possible contingencies" of whatever I'm worried about.

For pornography, the dynamic has changed in our culture. The rise of digital technology has weaponized pornography. It promises to guarantee anonymity. More than that, digital pornography now exists in such a way that a person can easily feel as though he or she is "accidentally" arriving there. In older days, one rarely can imagine a situation where one would, in the course of running errands, find that one had suddenly ended up in an X-rated theater. Now, one site can be clicked to the next so fast that one can almost feel as though one is arriving in these places with no planned-out will to do so. The anonymity and ease of this technology have contributed to its ubiquity, a ubiquity shored up by a popular culture in which characters in film and television often joke about porn as a routine matter of life.

But the problem is not merely external. A pornographic world would have no pull at all if not for the fact of fallen flesh. By "the flesh," the Bible does not mean the body, as though bodily reality is itself the issue. By "the flesh," the Bible means those aspects of our creaturely reality that are not yet subdued by the kingship of God. There's a reason why the allure of pornography feels different for many people than some other temptations they face. That's because sexuality itself often feels "wild" and uncontained. Of course it does. God designed you, after you are called to the marriage covenant, for sexual union. That's how God's image-bearing species continues to exist on the earth, because there is a strong pull to "leave father and mother" and to cleave to one another as one flesh (Gen. 2:24).

Pornography appeals first to this good and created longing, but twists it outside the covenant in which we were created to be in communion, naked and not ashamed (Gen. 2:25). In pornography, sexual desire is treated as a mere biological itch, rather than a drive toward communion. In pornography, masturbatory aloneness, with the nakedness of another as a tool to be used, replaces the one-flesh union designed precisely because it was not good that we be alone (Gen. 2:18). If we are driven by the Spirit, we are driven toward God and toward fellowship with one another. If we walk according to the flesh, our appetites start to control us. Pornography promises to address a real longing with a fake answer.

Now, this makes perfectly good sense if one accepts the reigning theory of what sexuality is all about. One of the reasons popular culture now treats pornography as a more-or-less natural part of human sexuality is because we don't recognize, culturally, what sexuality is all about. If sexual arousal is simply a biological urge toward orgasm, then, it could be reasoned, whatever gets one to orgasm is morally neutral, provided it doesn't violate some other overriding principle, such as consent.

The problem is not, first of all, that we approve the marketing of sex in the pornography industry, but, before all of that, we see all sex as essentially masturbatory. One seeks a "partner" with whom to have intercourse, but the sexual mechanics are often a quid pro quo of orgasm-for-orgasm, with "intimacy" meaning, "If I'm fulfilled sexually, I won't leave you." Such intimacy is, of course, no intimacy at all.

What the pornography industry gets right is just how strong the pull to sexual union is. Those who seek to regulate their sexual impulses soon find that such a project often makes them feel far more powerless than the willpower it takes to stick to a diet regime or a workout routine. Why?

A Darwinian reading of the cosmos would tell us, of course, that this is because the drive to sexual union is the pulse of the universe itself. Those with the drive to procreate are the ones who reproduce, and thus life churns on. In this view, pornography is as natural as can be, especially for men, hardwired as they are to seek novelty in order to spread their seed as widely as possible, ensuring the survival of the species. In this rendering, monogamy is what is artificial. Pornography uses technology in order to

Being married to one person at a time

provide the ever-expanding harem of new and different women a man "needs," all without jeopardizing the family his children need to grow up securely with both parents. The pornography can also, the pop-Darwinians might tell us, save families and individuals from the consequences, such as sexually transmitted disease, that "real" sex can bring. Even so, no culture can actually live with this vision of sexuality, at least not long term. Notice the way that our culture's songs and films and poems celebrate love, as something much more than biological instinct. Indeed, love might be the one thing even the most secularized culture sees as, in its own way, "spiritual."

The Christian account of sexuality, though, is very different. Sex is more than just a matter of the physics of two bodies interacting with one another. Our emotional involvement, at the thought, for instance, of sexual betrayal by a spouse or partner, is something more than just protecting the gene pool. The Bible tells us that sexual intercourse is not primarily about hormones and mechanics. In fact, sexual intercourse is not merely about forming or strengthening connections between two human beings. Sexual intercourse is, instead, a drama, pointing past itself, past humanity, past nature itself, toward the mystery of the universe—the gospel.

The apostle Paul warns often against sexual immorality, as does Jesus before him. But these warnings are not grounded in the idea that sex is unclean, nor are they grounded merely in the consequences of violating sexual boundaries. Jesus affirmed the creational norm of the union between one man and one woman, in lifelong covenant with one another (Mark 10:6–9), in contrast with both divorce and *porneia*, or sexual immorality (Matt. 19:9).

In the New Testament era, of course, there were no Internet sites, pornographic or otherwise. There was erotic dancing (see Herodias's daughter). And there was prostitution, both of the sort with which we are familiar and temple prostitution. Paul appealed to the Christians in Corinth about the temptation to pay for sexual activity disconnected from covenantal union. That, of course, is precisely what happens with pornography. "Actors" are paid to perform sexual acts for someone else's gratification. The Corinthians could easily dismiss this as a kind of "boys will be boys" matter of answering a biological urge. The Spirit, though, through the apostle defined this immorality as much more, more even than just a bad witness for Christ to the outside world (although it was certainly that). Rather, the one who joined himself to a prostitute was participating in something more than just a physical reality. He was joining Christ to this prostitute, since the body is the temple of the Holy Spirit (1 Cor. 6:19). Sexual immorality isn't just bad for marriages; it is the desecration of a holy place. This pull toward immorality is deeply spiritual, in participation with spirits quite different from the Holy Spirit of God.

That, of course, brings us to the Devil. Western people tend to be skeptical of unseen evil beings, dismissing such concerns as superstition. Sadly, many Western Christians unintentionally adopt this sort of dangerous demythologizing of the darker angels. Most cultures though, of whatever religion, have recognized some invisible reality around us that is personal and destructive. The Bible defines this reality, and warns us to "resist the devil" (James 4:7). The pull to temptation, whether to pornography or to some other act of self-destruction, can feel so bewildering precisely because it is, quite literally, bedeviling. This is spiritual warfare.

This wrestling with principalities and powers at the level of immorality is because, again, sexuality isn't just about the firing of nerve endings. The sexual union, within the marital bond, points beyond itself to a mystery, a mystery revealed in the New Testament as the union of Christ with His church (Eph. 5:32). That's why the Devil cares about it in the first place. The Devil-haunted cosmos wouldn't care about our marriage (present or future) or your sexual integrity as a single Christian if it were simply about consequences, real as they are. These forces despise the gospel pictured in living and breathing form in the sexual union of husband and wife in covenant with one another before the face of God.

All sexual immorality—whether non-marital sex or technologically engineered trafficking in lust—seeks to displace the presentation of this mystery with a presentation of another counter-gospel. They want to put us out of our mystery. That's why the pull to pornography is stronger than just managing it with a few web filters and some accountability groups (although these can be helpful tools).

The gospel addresses pornography, first of all, by showing you what your sexuality is, and calling on you to seek the Spirit to rightly order it under the lordship of Christ. The gospel also, though, frees you by unshackling you from the shame that would keep you captive, whether to actual pornography or the pornography of your own mind's making. One of the first consequences of our ancestral sin was that the man and the woman were now disconnected from one another, ashamed of their nakedness. Pornography does this with rampant efficiency.

I cannot count how many marriages have grown numb and dead, because the pornography in one spouse's life has burned over the erotic aspects needed for genuine intimacy. Many of these persons would rather masturbate to an image than to make love to a real spouse, and many will say it's because the intimacy feels too intimate, too "awkward." That ancestral sin also, though, caused sin before God. God comes to the garden and asks, "Adam, where are you?" and "What have you done?" The human creatures cower behind the coverings they have made for themselves, from the very same stuff that they used to fall in the first place—vegetation.

If we will confront what the pornography culture is doing to our own congregations, we must address the way the gospel speaks to shame. That means seeing that the Devil works first through a kind of shamelessness—the idea that there is no God who sees or knows. That's especially easy when what is happening is in a darkened room, alone. But then the Devil works by applying shame ruthlessly. The person is told, by his own conscience, that no matter how routine this sin appears, there is something deeply disordered. The whole course of this world then convinces this person that he or she must hide from view, especially from God and often from oneself. The gospel can and must upend all of that.

A gospel approach requires pastors and teachers within the church who will speak about pornography. Some congregations are too squeamish for this. They clutch their pearls in shocked indignation when pornography is mentioned because it is too sensitive for younger ears to hear. Notice, though, how the Bible is not afraid at all to confront serious issues—including those that make us squirm in the pews next to our kids. If the Bible is the whole counsel of God, the whole people of God need the whole Bible. And if the gospel is good news for sinners, then every sin must be called to repentance and every sin must be offered the merciful covering of the blood of Christ.

The gospel tells us, "If we walk in the light as he himself is in the light, we have fellowship with one another, and the blood of Jesus his Son cleanses us from all sin" (1 John 1:7). We tend to think of light as airy and non-threatening (as in the dismissive phrase "sweetness and light"). From a gospel frame, though, light is painful. "And this is the judgment," Jesus said. "The light has come into the world, and people loved darkness rather than the light because their deeds were evil" (John 3:19). Light exposes, just as the voice of God does with the man and the woman of the garden.

Left to ourselves, we would prefer to keep our shadows out of our own consciousness, and certainly out of the view of God. But the gospel is better news than that. Churches should teach what the Bible says about lust and immorality, directly in the context of pornography. Churches should also explicitly state that there are, almost without doubt, men and women in the room in various degrees of temptation toward slavery to pornography.

If we don't, those who find themselves walking further and further down this road will conclude that they are beyond the reach of the gospel. They will conclude perhaps that such matters are "only human," and thus wrongly assume their sin is too trivial to affect them spiritually now or before the judgment seat of Christ. Or, more likely, they will sit in shame and hiddenness, believing they are too "perverted" to be loved or forgiven by God. Our gospel tells us, "If we confess our sins, he is faithful and righteous to forgive us our sins and to cleanse us from all unrighteousness" (1 John 1:9). All of that is true and necessary.

We must acknowledge sin as sin, and we must also see God's offer of forgiveness and cleansing. All of that, though, requires one to come out from hiding, to be naked in your vulnerability before God—and to be healed.

It is not enough to know that you are sinful. Judas knew that, and his conscience drove him to suicide in the potter's field. You must, like Simon Peter, not only see your sin, but also be willing to stand before the Jesus you've betrayed, to be washed by Him, to be forgiven by Him.

For all I know, you may be reading this right now while you are losing a battle with pornography. If you're a Christian, you know that you've been called to ongoing repentance, but you find yourself perpetually tempted by pornography. This temptation may be with you your entire life. The answer is to confront the question of who you are. You are joined to Christ. His Spirit is in you, able to overcome your appetites and your stumbling blocks.

You may have such a vulnerability that you should protect yourself from yourself, even beyond routine protections such as Internet filters. You may need to remove all devices capable of conveying pornography from your home, if you feel too vulnerable at the moment to handle such. It may be that you need a group of others with whom you can talk about this, Christians with the same wrestling match. Ask your church for such a ministry; tell them you need others to help bear your burdens (Gal. 6:2).

But, more than that, the antidote to this and other temptations is the priesthood of Christ, the One who was tempted before us, and who right now is interceding for you before the Father (Heb. 2:17–18). You may feel ashamed before Him. But Jesus is not shocked or surprised. He knew your sins and struggles when He sent the gospel to you in the first place. He is no more ashamed of you than He was of the sinners with whom He ate in His earthly ministry, or of His bumbling, sinning disciples. He is also not willing to leave you in the mire of whatever captivity you find yourself in.[5]

Pay attention to your life. When are you most vulnerable to the temptation toward pornography? That should tell you something about your need for communion with God, through Christ by the Spirit, at those points in your life. When you feel the pull toward pornography, do not fear. Recognize the danger. This is a predator, seeking to destroy you (1 Pet. 5:8). Cry out in those moments, "Lord, have mercy on me!" just as you would if you were in a plane plummeting toward the ground. You may not know what to pray. That's why you have a High Priest praying for you, and a Spirit within you driving you toward utterances sometimes too deep, and too raw, for words (Rom. 8:26–27). Find a friend with whom you can be vulnerable enough to call and say, "I'm tempted to access pornography; can you pray with me now?" That will be difficult to do, but that's precisely what the Devil fears.

It may be that you, or someone you love, have a background in pornography. Maybe you, or this person, are now free from pornography. Maybe you are constantly on the precipice of falling backward into it. You may have a conscience that is burdened down with guilt and shame. At the cross, Jesus willingly bore our guilt and shame, all of it. God knew about your sexual immorality *before* He sent Jesus to live and die for you. It is, after all, while we were "still sinners" that "Christ died for us" (Rom. 5:6). If you don't cling to that, you will believe that somehow you are especially freakish, and you will return back to the pigsty of pornography, for fear of being rejected at the Father's house (Luke 15:11–32).

All of this brings us back to 42nd Street. Frederick Buechner wrote that his response to the pornotopia around him was fear—fear that he would get lost there and never find his way out. "I was scared that everybody I saw coming toward me down the crowded sidewalk—old and young, well dressed and ragged, innocent and corrupt—was in danger of getting lost," he wrote. "I was scared that the world itself was as lost as it was mad. And of course in a thousand ways it is."[6] The scariness of pornography doesn't confront us now on sidewalks but on digital media platforms, with technologies on the way that we can surely not even imagine.

Whatever changes, though, the primal human fear is still there, the fear of getting lost with no way out of the thicket of your own fallen desire. The world, the flesh, and the Devil will tell you it doesn't matter. And then these same forces will tell you that you are too far gone, without hope, without remedy, and lost. But Jesus came to seek and to save that which was lost. Pornography is powerful because it appeals to something more than glands. Pornography is powerful because it presents a counter-gospel, a momentary burst of what promises to be "good news" of freedom from boredom or from alienation or from self-hatred. You do not have to be lost in your Internet history. You do not have to go where this road will take you, right to the doors of death and hell. The gospel can shake you from deception and free you from accusation. That, and that alone, is good news, even for a scary, bustling, and sad pornographic world.

Discussion Questions

1. In what ways do the world, the flesh, and the Devil work together to encourage a pornographic culture?
2. How has pornography become "weaponized"? In what ways has technology removed many of the social stigmas associated with viewing pornographic material? Why is the promise of anonymity a lie?
3. How does the gospel speak to shame? How does the Bible help us address issues that make us squirm?
4. When are you most vulnerable to falling into pornography? What gospel truths can help you overcome these temptations?

CHAPTER 3

How Should the Christian Live?

Courtney Reissig

I REMEMBER MY FIRST ENCOUNTER WITH PORNOGRAPHY. I was at someone's house going to the bathroom and I saw a *Playboy* on the seat. Curiosity got the better of me and I looked and looked and looked. In an instant, my innocent mind was catapulted to a world I never should have entered, and could never come back from. Fast-forward a few years, and I would regularly find myself sitting in my high school computer class (pre-security filters) viewing pornographic images with my friends (male and female) just for laughs. As a young woman, I took in a steady diet of romantic comedies and sex-filled movies that confused my understanding of sex and body image even further. I'm not a victim of pornography. I wasn't even "addicted" to it. I just didn't turn away from it when it presented itself before Christ saved me. In a lot of ways, you could say that I am a product of the pornography culture we find ourselves in today.

One of the primary criticisms Christians raise against pornography is that porn hurts women. That is absolutely true. But implicit in that line of reasoning is an assumption that women are the passive victims of pornography, and that's just not always the case. To begin to respond to a pornography culture, we will need to make some admissions about pornography and its effect on us, starting with addressing the men *and* the women who are enslaved to its oppressive power.

Reporting from a study done by the Barna Group, Jonathan Merritt cites these statistics on pornography use.

> When they speak about pornography with friends, 90 percent of teens (ages 13 to 17) and 96 percent of young adults (ages 18 to 24) say they do so in a neutral, accepting, or encouraging way. Only one in 20 young adults and one in 10 teens say their friends think viewing pornography is a bad thing.

He goes on to say:

While men have traditionally consumed pornography at a much higher rate than women, it appears that females (particularly younger ones) are starting to catch up. Thirty-three percent of women ages thirteen to twenty-four seek out porn at least once per month.[7]

And to go even further, when it comes to sexting, 66 percent of teens claim they have sent at least one sexually explicit message (the majority of the senders being female), while 41 percent claim they have received at least one such message. All of this to say, we must acknowledge that we have a widespread issue on our hands that goes well beyond our men's groups and "just say no" campaigns.

This Is a Human Issue, Not a Men's Issue

Perhaps you are reading this and were surprised by my admission at the beginning of this chapter. I am a woman. Women don't talk much about pornography and its death-like grip on our psyches. Sure, we talk about how it affects our marriages, our sons, how men view us, but rarely do we talk publicly about the fact that we are also consumers. But we are. Some women are drawn into pornography by a boyfriend or spouse or even curiosity. But others walk right into pornography apart from the influence of any men in their lives. They look at it because they want to.

While the tide is slowly shifting, many women are simply unwilling to admit to viewing or having viewed pornography. For some reason, there is a collective silence on the issue in women's literature.

Let's break that silence.

Statistically, as we've already seen, women are just as likely as men to engage in some form of porn consumption. This is not new, especially if you consider the abundant supply of grocery store romance novels, the enduring popularity of sex-driven soap operas (though the viewership is finally waning), and the constant production of movies and books designed to appeal to a woman's sex drive. The marketplace is flooded with pornography. And women have been consumers of pornographic material for a long time; we just haven't called it that.

In fact, a pro-porn mantra is a hallmark of third-wave feminism, the feminism of my generation. We are a far cry from the feminists of old, linking arms with the Christian coalitions to fight against pornography. Now we have men and women of all ages and backgrounds linking arms to say that pornography really isn't all that bad if that is what you want to do. This so-called "pro-sex feminism" is considered pro-porn, when it is used as a form of displaying female enjoyment of sex and empowerment.

In a debate in *Ms. Magazine*, one pro-porn feminist said this about the value of pornography:

> Many anti-pornography feminists believe that porn is an apparatus of the patriarchy that reduces women to sex objects and is a part of the systematic oppression and degradation of women, but this claim robs the performers of control over their bodies and shames them for participating in an industry that provides them with financial stability and the opportunity to explore their sexuality. As feminist writer Ellen Willis once said, "The claim that 'pornography is violence against women' was code for the neo-Victorian idea that men want sex and women endure it."[8]

So, while we used to come together to fight pornography and its harmful effects on women, third-wave feminism has changed all of that. In theory, women can be as aggressive, sexual, and raunchy as men desire them to be, and they are none the weaker. If they are the ones putting it out there, they are the ones who are in control. If a woman wants to send a naked picture of herself to her boyfriend—or even more blatant—post it on the Internet, she is not a victim, she is empowered. In fact, women are influencing the pornography industry at some of the highest levels. According to author Ariel Levy, even *Playboy* is no longer simply a men's magazine. She explains:

Playboy is case in point. Playboy's image has everything to do with its pajama-clad, septuagenarian,
babe-magnet founder, Hugh Hefner, and the sur-
real world of celebrities, multiple "girlfriends" and
nonstop bikini parties he's set up around himself.
But in actuality, Playboy is a company largely run
by women. Hefner's daughter Christie is the chair-
man and CEO of Playboy Enterprises. The CFO is
a middle-aged mother named Linda Havard. The
Playboy Foundation (which has supported the ERA
and abortion rights among other progressive causes)
is run by Cleo Wilson, an African-American for-
mer civil-rights activist. A woman named Marilyn
Grabowski produces more than half the magazines
photo features . . . That women are now doing
this to themselves isn't some kind of triumph, it's
depressing.[9]

Did you catch all those women? While men are still the larg-
est consumers of actual pornography, we cannot escape the fact
that this issue is far more inclusive than we had once thought.

This changes the way we deal with the issue. It changes the
way a pastor preaches about pornography, how a women's ministry director counsels someone affected by pornography, and
the way parents address pornography in their homes. No one is
safe from pornography's reach, and the sooner we admit that,

the sooner we can minister to people who may be lurking in the shadows, afraid to admit their sin.

But connected to the issue of pornography use comes the more fundamental issue mentioned above, porn actually does hurt women. Of course, it also hurts men, but women are severely marginalized and dehumanized by the pornography use of both men and women. Porn is a human issue because it affects everyone around you, even when you engage in what feels like a very personal and private activity. Porn is not just between the viewer and the people on the screen or in the magazine. It reaches much further. It changes who we are. It changes how we think. And it changes how we see those around us.

Porn teaches us to view people as objects. It reduces sex to something cold, emotionless, and mechanical. And as the first generation of young people who grew up with access to online porn-on-demand is coming of age, we are watching the consequences unfold before our eyes. Though they have manifested in a number of ways, perhaps the most troubling, and most pressing, is the stunning inability of college-age men to understand what consent is, and the apparent inability of college-age women to clearly say "no" when it comes to unwanted sexual intimacy.

All across the country, college administrators are attempting to grapple with the problem of sexual assault. One of the ways they are tackling this is by hosting "consent classes" where they teach the meaning of "yes" and "no" when it comes to sex. Raised on a steady diet of pornography, college-age men and women are having a hard time navigating the waters of sexual activity in the shadow of a pornography culture.

In an episode of *This American Life*, one of the most popular radio programs and podcasts in the history of the broadcasting, listeners were given a window into one such consent class, learning anything from where the young men present learned about sex (from pornography and their friends) and their confusion over the need to perpetually gain consent from the women they are having sex with (all throughout the sexual experience).[10]

This is not unique to suburban, middle-class students with too much time on their hands. It is everywhere. And this is only the tip of the iceberg. Studies have shown that prolonged exposure to pornography has devastating effects on the way an individual views sex, his or her sexual partner, and even human interaction. In short, prolonged porn use creates monsters who only think of themselves. How do you help a young man register the word "no" or "I don't like that" when his first and only experiences with sex have been in the context of a professionally orchestrated sexual act that he views alone on a screen? If women never say "no" in porn, then how can they truly mean it when it happens in real life? How do you teach a young girl that the images she sees on her friend's phone at school are not real, that women don't really look like the images on the screen? How do you teach a husband not to expect his wife to perform just like the porn stars do?

Porn is not just about men and their lustful hearts. And the problem can't be solved by just thinking about something else when you are tempted to look at porn again. The problem of porn has become so much more than that. We are all pornographers now. To varying degrees, we are all part of its curse.

Addressing the problem of porn will require us to rightly estimate the scope of the problem. Our solutions must concentrate on the root issues, not the aftereffects. For starters, we must see women as human beings instead of objects to be desired. We must recognize that women are just as drawn to pornography's allure as men. We must accept that we have all been affected by pornography in some capacity, whether as consumers, participants, or victims. We must admit that pornography affects us all. It is not limited to the individual. It includes every single person involved in creating, distributing, and consuming it. Yet it reaches beyond even that. It permeates our culture and distorts our understanding of personhood, sexuality, and intimacy. Porn's reach is broad and its effects are destructive. This is not a men's issue; it is a human one. If we hope to make any progress in combatting pornography, we must begin with that admission.

We Are All Pornographers Now

A number of years ago, while working in youth ministry, I heard about a student who was suspended from a Christian school for sending a naked picture of herself to a male student. Of course, the private picture, intended only for him, was then sent to the entire football team. In some states, this very act is considered a crime—child pornography—and those involved could be subject to felony prosecution. The advent of technology that we can hold in the palms of our hands has made the problem of pornography more difficult to diagnose and combat. The stupidity of high school lust used to be limited to things like showing too much skin to the guys under the bleachers. While still sinful and foolish, the only record of the act would be the memory etched in the boys' minds. But this is not the case any longer. In a lot of ways, the rapid advancement of technology in our culture is moving faster that the mechanisms we have to protect those who are using it. And, of course, pornography is moving right along with it.

The sad reality is that pornography is no longer isolated. It isn't relegated to sex stores on the side of the freeway; it's waiting for us in the privacy of our own homes. It used to be that you had to walk into a strip club, buy a magazine over the counter, or walk into a pornographic movie store to get your hands (or eyes) on porn. But not anymore. Porn is as ubiquitous in our world as high fructose corn syrup. It's everywhere, in everything, and subtly (and not so subtly) wreaking havoc on all who come in contact with it. From watching it on our screens, to texting it on our phones, to seeing it on the magazines at the checkout stand, it's everywhere. Soft porn to hard porn, amateur to professional, we are all in some way pornographers now.

Maybe you read that last line and are thinking: *I'm not a pornographer! I've never once sent a naked picture of myself, let alone viewed explicit images.* Perhaps you haven't watched explicit pornography, but I wonder if you have ever watched a sex scene in a movie? What about the commercials for a lingerie store? What about a magazine that tells you how to be good in bed? Until we reject the belief that porn only exists in strip clubs, X-rated theaters, and the dark corners of the Internet, we will not succeed in fighting pornography. It is pervasive and it is everywhere. Until we stop viewing porn use as an outside-of-our-circle issue, we will not have the guts or the discernment to face it head-on. We are all pornographers because we have all participated in some part of this pro-porn culture. Actually fighting pornography will require us to admit this reality, repent of our complicity, and finally call porn use what it is—lust.

Call It What It Is

Perhaps the greatest source of victory for those stuck in a world of pornography is to call it what the Bible calls it—lust. The context for viewing it has changed, but it is old-fashioned lust repackaged and put within a shiny, personal handheld device. Jesus said that if you even look at a woman with lustful intent you have committed adultery in your heart (Matt. 5:27–28). Pornography use is the epitome of lust. The Song of Solomon reminds us not to awaken love until its proper time (Song of Sol. 2:7; 8:4). There is a time and place for sex; anything outside of that is lust.

When we call pornography addiction lust, when we respond to a pro-porn culture with the Bible's language, we have a better hope for recovery, because we know the antidote to sin. It's Jesus. The Bible reminds us that there is no temptation that has overtaken us that is not common to us all (1 Cor. 10:13). We are not fighting a battle against sin that is unique to twenty-first-century America; we are fighting a battle that has been around since Adam and Eve fell into sin and took us all with them. This should give us even greater encouragement to fight the fight against pornography because we know that every sin has been paid for, in full, by Jesus on the cross (Rom. 4:25; 1 Pet. 3:18).

Diagnose Yourself

Maybe you have read this far and think that pornography still doesn't affect you. It's an issue for other people, but certainly not for you.

Perhaps that is true.

But I wonder if it is possible to see, accurately, how pervasive pornography is in our culture and still respond in that way. We shouldn't hide from it, nor should we pretend that it isn't affecting us. We are all in some way influenced by its lies and its allure. So before going any further, here are some questions to ask yourself about whether or not pornography is affecting your life:

1. Do you view sex as an overly emotional experience? Do you view sex as an always pleasurable experience?
2. Do you think about your own pleasure when you think about sex?
3. Do you think the perfect female body is one free from stretch marks, extra skin, or any blemish?
4. Do you think men instinctively know what women want in bed? Do you think women instinctively know what men want in bed?
5. Are you tempted to try things that make you feel uncomfortable sexually because you think it will make your sexual experience more enjoyable or more over-the-top?
6. Do you feel discouraged or defeated when sex is not everything you hoped for every single time?

7. Are you unable to feel "in the mood" without thinking about an image you have seen previously? Do you find yourself drawn back to these images during sex?

These are just a handful of questions, and I admit, some of them can be rather uncomfortable to voice out loud, but they are worth thinking about. Perhaps you have never viewed pornography, but maybe you have seen one too many sex scenes in the movies you have watched, or read about sex too much in women's magazines. The proliferation of all things sex in our culture is directly related to our struggle against pornography. This is one reason that it is so difficult to combat its power over our own minds and the minds of those we love.

So how can Christians fight against it? How do we live faithfully in a porn-filled culture? Here are a few suggestions:

Have a Healthy View of Sex

This may seem obvious, but if pornography presents a distorted view of sex, the answer to its influence can't simply be, "Just say no." We must put forward a healthy alternative to the feeble view of sex that pornography offers us.

It has been said that the constant refrain in our churches for young people to save themselves for marriage has only made our young people confused and afraid of sex. People enslaved to pornography and people who are victims of its grip need more than horror stories and warnings of sexual brokenness and dysfunc-tion. They need to see *why* the vision of sexuality offered by por-nography is not God's plan in the first place. They need a healthy and biblical view of sex. They need to see God's beautiful design for marital intimacy in order to fully comprehend the ugliness of pornography and lust. They need to see that God did create them for pleasure, but for a pleasure that finds its joy in the good of another. But most important, they need to see that by finding their joy in the pleasure of another they are actually worshipping God. All good gifts, even the gift of sex, are designed to point us to the giver of that gift. Pornography strips the gift of sex from the God who created it. We can channel the good desires for sex that so many people have away from pornography by showing them that those desires are driving them to the only one who can truly satisfy them completely—our Creator.

This goes beyond church campaigns to celebrate sex. We don't need to adopt the world's ideology when it comes to think-ing positively about sex. Instead, we must present God's healthy view of sex to the people in our churches and under our care, not so they can be as sex-experienced as the world around them, but so they can catch a glimpse of God's intentional, perfect, and loving design for His people. They need to see husbands and wives loving each other in sickness and in health. They need to see husbands finding their wives beautiful even after decades of life, years of childbearing, physical illness, and gravity takes its toll on their wives' bodies. They need to see wives enjoying their husbands when he can't do the things he used to do or even can't physically engage in the sexual act any longer. They need to see the ebbs and flows of life that shape a marriage and strengthen a family. They need to see people enjoying God even when the gift of sex is not all they hoped it would be or even absent altogether. Only when we present sex within the context of covenant-keeping love, within the context of sacrificial service regardless of circumstances, within the context of unconditional affection when the storms of life take you where you don't want to go, and within the context of it being a good gift meant to push us toward God, will we begin to combat the self-seeking, idolatrous nature of pornography.

Have a Healthy Understanding of Shame

But we can't end there. Within the cycle of pornography lies a very real struggle with shame and guilt that often feels impossible to break. Especially for the Christian, a life enslaved to pornography involves a lot of vowing to never look again only to be met with failure and shame. In some ways, the shame one feels over his or her sin is a good thing. Shame takes us places, either to despair or transformation. But shame is not the goal. Coupled with a healthy understanding of sex, we must also have a healthy understanding of shame or guilt.

The apostle Paul understood this temptation for those who are confronted with their sin. After writing a letter to the Corinthians about their sin, Paul encouraged them that the sorrow they felt over their sin served its purpose. It led them to repentance (2 Cor. 7:8–13). And not only repentance, but a transformed life (vv. 11–12). We naturally will feel shame over the sin that we commit, and this includes the sin of pornography. But our shame shouldn't sideline us. Our shame serves a good and hopeful purpose—to lead us to Christ.

Have a Healthy Solution for Redemption

All of this talk about the effects of pornography and turning from pornography would be in vain if we didn't point to our Savior. The best-laid plans to turn from any sin are futile if we don't have Christ, who cleanses us from all unrighteousness (1 John 1:9) and provides us with a means of change (John 14:26). The hope for change after sensing guilt over your sinful use of pornography or your lustful thoughts is to first repent of your sin and then look to Christ, who is your advocate before a holy God (1 John 2:1), your faithful brother who sympathizes with you in weakness and temptation (Heb. 4:15), and your perfect High Priest who atones for your sin in its entirety.

The lie of our sex-crazed culture is that you need more of it in order to be a fully functioning human. The more you look, act, and lust, the more your insatiable soul desires to be filled again and again and again. But the truth of God's Word says that in Christ all of your thirsts for glory are filled by the God who knows you better than you know yourself and satisfies more deeply than any fleeting image ever could.

The response to a pornography culture begins with first acknowledging our place in its influence, spread, and appeal and then turning to the Bible for a reorientation of our view of sex, shame, and the gospel.

Pornography isn't going anywhere. If anything, it is going to continue to become even more mainstream than it is now. But as Christians, we do not need to resign ourselves to its dominion over us. We can live as aliens and strangers in a world that sees sex as a commodity. We can fill our thirsty souls by celebrating and experiencing God's good design for sex. This is now a problem for all of us to address. But despite the power pornography wields today, we know that Christ has already secured its defeat.

Discussion Questions

1. How have you been influenced by the pornography culture?
2. When confronted with your sexual sin, do you tend toward a "godly grief" or "worldly grief"? How does

your response to your sin shape your relationships and your own walk with God?

3. What can you do to encourage a healthy view of sex in your own life and in the lives of those you influence? How do you see the culture influencing or distorting your view of sex?

4

How Should the Church Engage?

Jared C. Wilson

ROGER AND EVELYN SAT UNEASILY IN THE TWO CUSHY GUEST chairs in my pastoral study.[11] Evelyn gnawed on her lower lip and stared at the floor. Roger stared at me like a deer in the headlights. What they were about to share with me was something I had heard countless times throughout nearly twenty years of ministry, but for them, it was new, it was fresh, it was in some sense "the end of the world."

Roger had a porn problem. He was late fifties, several decades into a blue-collar career, and he had a nose-to-the-grindstone, tough-guy, no-nonsense way about him. He was a guy who whooped every challenge he faced. Except this one.

It was sports websites that had done him in, he explained. He just wanted to check the score of the ballgames, but the sidebar ads were baited too well, and he ended up just making one or two extra clicks to see whatever lurid things they promised.

Evelyn was disgusted. And deeply hurt. She could not see the appeal, could not see why her allegedly mature Christian husband could be so persistently interested in pictures and videos so obviously gross. And she couldn't understand why she wasn't enough. She worried he'd grown tired of her, that her age was diminishing her attractiveness to him. Roger's porn use triggered the deepest-seated insecurity in his wife—that she wasn't good enough, that she wasn't lovely, that she wasn't worthy.

I don't recall how Roger's browsing history was exposed, but whatever transpired in the aftermath of this revelation had brought them to their pastor for help. Roger was looking for a good talking-to and a checklist of things he might obey to demonstrate his repentance. Evelyn was hoping he'd get a good talking-to as well, but mostly she wanted some kind of explanation, and some kind of comfort. Why would Roger do this? And how could she (and they) get past it?

Whether from past church experience or simply from their own sense of the gravity of the situation, they sat before me broken and burdened, apparently expecting some kind of hellfire and brimstone sermon on holiness.

I looked at them both softly, a gentle smile on my face. I had a few things to share with them, but the most important (in that moment) was this—you are not alone.

Demystifying the Problem

One of the biggest problems the church has with pornography lies with just how covertly it treats the issue. Now, this is completely understandable on a couple of levels. First, pornography is the graphic depiction (whether in writing, pictures, or movie images) of sexual acts, and of course those who are born-again followers of Jesus Christ understand that sex is intended to be a private act reserved only for a husband and wife. Sexual immorality is a shameful thing, so it's only natural we would hesitate to speak of it so publicly. Even many who are not converted instinctively understand that sexual intercourse is a private kind of intimacy and that pornography is not something for public display and discussion.

Second, there was a time when porn was reserved for the shadier corners of our culture. Once upon a time, anyone interested in seeing this kind of material had to travel to a seedy part of town and enter a darkened theater. Maybe people passed around magazines. In any event, the use of pornography was somewhat marginalized, something unbecoming of polite society and thought only to appeal to a minute number of society's perverts. These are the primary reasons the church has struggled to speak to the problem of pornography.

But we can't ignore the subject any longer. Churches cannot carry on as if porn is some marginal problem in the life of their communities. For one thing, the advent of the home video market and cable television radically increased the availability of illicit material. Porn began to creep out of our culture's societal corrals and invade more and more homes. And of course, once the Internet age dawned, bringing with it the proliferation of personal computers and handheld devices with easy and instant connection to the World Wide Web, the porn virus became an outright plague.

The first and primary way the church must respond to the problem of pornography is to admit that she herself has this problem. It is not simply a sin *out there* committed by "those people." It's not limited to back alleys and red-light districts. It is in the bedrooms and hotel rooms and laptops and mobile devices of her own participants. And in fact, it is a sin that has been engaged in by more of the church's participants than not. You would be hard pressed to find a man living in the twenty-first century who hasn't struggled with porn use and certainly almost all men have had the opportunity to see it.

If we want to address the problem well, we have to demystify the use of pornography. Now, by "demystify," I don't mean justify, condone, acquiesce to, or otherwise downplay. I simply mean that we cannot adequately address a problem if we cannot honestly admit how common it is.

And it's not getting any less common. The age at which a male first sees pornography is getting younger and younger year after year, and porn use is a growing problem among women both young and old. It's time to dispense with the antiquated notion that pornography only tempts a certain kind of pervert of a certain age. No, in effect, it tempts *all of us*. (The widespread appeal among middle-aged and older women of the *Fifty Shades of Grey* book series and its growing number of knock-offs are just one sign of the increasing way porn is seen as mainstream.)

Understanding the incredible prevalence of the problem helps us to see how engaging the issue is no longer optional. But understanding the incredible prevalence of the problem also helps us to see how we ought to engage the issue in the first place. Because porn now appeals to men and women of all ages in all kinds of circumstances and in all places, we must make some important theological deductions about the problem.

For instance, in many church communities over the last several decades, sins like pornography use have essentially become earners of scarlet letters. Porn is seen by many as the unpardonable sin. But if we continue preaching, discipling, and counseling this way, we will soon find that we've excommunicated our church into oblivion! So after we've brought our perspective on the problem into the twenty-first century to see just how widespread it is, we then need to bring our discernment about the problem into mankind's earliest history to see just how universal it is.

Getting to the Root of the Problem

It confused Evelyn to hear that Roger's porn problem wasn't simply about sex. It confused her, because pornography is obviously and graphically about sex. But my counsel to them that difficult night included a deeper perspective on the issue that, in the end, she actually found somewhat encouraging.

See, porn use is only superficially about sexual gratification. Like all behavioral sin, however, porn use is about more than it appears. Like the sexual lust that fuels and feeds on pornography—and like all manner of sexual immorality—pornography is essentially about worship. There is something being trusted in to satisfy, to fulfill, to (of course) gratify in the pursuit and consumption of porn that runs deeper than sexual release. This is why, for instance, the porn addict finds that his tastes over time become coarser and coarser, why his pornographic preferences nearly always devolve into material that is "harder," more extreme, and frequently violent or otherwise more taboo-breaking. If it were simply about the physical release, the material that appealed at the first would always be enough. But we crave for more from the object of our worship, and as it fails to satisfy, we continue to look deeper and push further in search of fulfillment.

Secondarily, we discover that it's not just single men or married men in sexless marriages wrestling with the sin of pornography. This is what originally bothered Evelyn so much. She did not see herself as sexually unavailable to her husband. And while their sex life was certainly not as active or carefree as it had been in the early years of their marriage, she generally enjoyed sex with her husband and knew their intimacy was neither uncommon nor unsatisfactory.

To hear that Roger's susceptibility to porn had more to do with his own insufficient addressing of personal stress, fatigue, and anxiety than it did with his feelings about their marriage bed was an odd kind of relief. Underneath Roger's sin was a storm of feelings that made him particularly vulnerable to the lure of porn. He was getting older; a sort of mid-life crisis had set in, where he was facing the rather hard truth that he would never be as strong or as healthy as he had been before, which made him feel unattractive and undesirable. He also was under a lot of stress at work, a problem only exacerbated by the weariness of the long hours and an acute sense of not being in control.

None of these are excuses for using porn! It was important for Evelyn to hear that, just as it was important for Roger to hear

that. But attacking porn use must mean attacking the disposi-
tions that weaken our resistance to it in times of temptation.
When Roger felt tired and weak, his guard was down, and it
became easier to justify in the moment how using porn made
him (for each brief moment in time) feel young, desirable, and—
above all—in control.

The women in porn exist as objects eager to please, specially
tuned to the specific appetites of the man consuming them. They
(pretend to) enjoy it, and your wish is their command. Porn provides this heady rush of being known and being served. In that
sense, porn is no different from any sin. Every sinful act is the
product of a sinful belief, a disbelief in God. Sin is faithless. It is
how we demonstrate our distrust in God to satisfy us, comfort
us, or provide for us. When we sin, we are saying essentially,
"God, You cannot be trusted to meet my needs. Right now I
choose instead to trust *this*."

For the church to powerfully confront pornography, she
must understand that porn is not simply about sex. It's not unre-
lated, of course, but it's not essentially a sex problem. Porn is
essentially a worship problem. Thankfully, though, the Christian
church is actually the only God-ordained context for addressing
worship problems.

The Gospel Is the Antidote to Porn Use

The single most important thing a church can do to help combat the lure of pornography (and all kinds of sexual immorality) is make sure the gospel of Jesus Christ is the single most important thing about the church. If Paul is right in 2 Corinthians 3:18 that beholding the glory of Jesus transforms us, and if he is right in Titus 2:11–12 that it is *grace* that trains people to renounce ungodliness, and if he is right in Romans 2:4 that it is God's *kindness* that leads us to repentance—and of course, he is—then we cannot expect the routine work of reminding people of the law to do an adequate job. In countless other Bible passages, we see that it is only the gospel that solves our worship problem.

The commands of God are good and holy. Christians are not to ignore God's laws! And we ought to apply the Seventh Commandment (the prohibition of adultery) to the sin of porn use, as it encompasses much more than physical intercourse with a person one is not married to. But while the law is good, it is only good at what it's intended to do—reveal the standard by which we're to live and reveal our falling short of that standard. The law cannot empower us to obey itself. No, we need the Holy Spirit working through the grace of God for that. Grace is the only "thing" the Scripture refers to as *power*. So, Christians are not free from the commandments, only the condemnation that comes from them. In a way, we are both free from the law and free to the law. Now we can obey God with joy and gratitude without fear that when we mess up we will be unjustified.

Until we understand that the gospel is the doorway into freedom from sin, even our religious efforts will simply be rearranging idols. What we are facing, as we have seen, is *a worship problem*. If we are not walking according to the Spirit in the grace of God, all of our efforts to change, including religious efforts, become acts of self-worship conducted according to the flesh. We have to find our satisfaction in Christ; any other fulfillment we seek to replace the idolatry in porn will simply be another idol.

Porn Is Not Primarily a Sex Problem, but a Worship Problem

Sean was another man who came to me for counsel about a porn problem. Sean's wife was not a believer, and this was an endless source of grief to him. But she was also very cold to him. They had sex maybe once or twice a year. This was extremely difficult for him, as well. He missed the feeling of being delighted in. He desperately wanted his wife to be in love with him, and this was in fact a greater desire for him than simply sexual release. But in porn he had found the illusion of delight and a fleeting fulfillment of sexual release.

One thing we had to get to quickly in our times of discipleship together: his wife's love for him could not be the solution to his porn problem. In other words, while her demeanor toward him was certainly wrong, his choices could not be contingent upon her behavior. Even if she did reliably show love to him emotionally and physically, he should not be trusting in his wife's feelings for his own sense of approval and validation. Sean's wife had become his god; she was his functional savior. But even godly wives cannot meet this demand, which is why so many husbands of godly wives also fall prey to adulterous lusts. Until we replace the idol of porn with the glory of Jesus found only in the gospel, we will just be switching out one idol for another.

Thomas Chalmers was a fellow who understood this very well. In his classic essay "The Expulsive Power of a New Affection," Chalmers writes:

> It is quite in vain to think of stopping one of these
> pursuits in any way else, but by stimulating to
> another. In attempting to bring a worldly man, intent
> and busied with the prosecution of his objects, to
> a dead stand, we have not merely to encounter the
> charm which he annexes to these objects—but we
> have to encounter the pleasure which he feels in the
> very prosecution of them. It is not enough, then, that
> we dissipate the charm, by a moral, and eloquent,
> and affecting exposure of its illusiveness. You must

address to the eye of his mind another object, with a
charm powerful enough to dispossess the first of its
influences. . .[12]

In other words, Chalmers is saying that until a more powerful affection displaces the sinful affection (in this case, lust),
we will simply be replacing old sins with new ones. It's like the
addict who is proud of moving on from cocaine to alcohol. Later,
Chalmers goes on to extol the gospel of Jesus Christ as the only
means of subverting worldly affections. Until we have truly
tasted and seen that God is good, until we have been set free by
the free gift of God's grace in Jesus' sinless life, sacrificial death,
and glorious resurrection, we will simply be trading in one slave
master for another, and thus never truly be free.

Internet filters, accountability partners, confessions and
admissions, and rigorous living can all be good things. But only
the gospel gets to the root of the porn problem, because only the
gospel presents to us One so glorious He makes all other objects
of worship pale, putrid things by comparison.

The Pastor's Role

So how do the church's pastors and other leaders and disci-
plers fit into all of this? If the crucial point of action is pointing to
the gospel as the antidote to porn use, what are practical means
of doing this? Here are a few suggestions:

1. Sensitive Treatment of Those Who Are Hurt

When a married man (or woman) confesses to porn use and asks for help, the pastor should be particularly sensitive to the wounds of the confessor's spouse. Many times they will feel as if they are not enough, as if they have somehow enabled the sin, which is very much a sin against them. A pastor must provide gentle counsel here and much gospel comfort. One person's sin is nobody else's fault, and especially in situations like this, we must absolutely avoid leaving a wounded spouse with the impression that they are somehow responsible. Don't further victimize victims.

2. Counsel toward the Root

Filters and accountability software and the like are good things and should be employed. This helps with transparency, with bringing a repentant sinner into the light, where sin is less likely to grow. But while these restrictions are good things, they do not get under the surface. In our counseling and discipling of those struggling with porn, we have to help them identify their moments of weakness and vulnerability. Ask them what circumstances (time of day, emotional state, events) are typically present when they most feel tempted. What do these conditions say about how lust is appealing to them? Help your counselee to identify and address the "perfect storm" for their susceptibility to porn. This goes further toward their being on guard against it and preemptively fleeing from sin.

3. Decoding Sexual Perversions

This is an especially complex work of discernment. Obviously most pastors and even biblical counselors are not clinical psychologists, but sound pastoral counseling should often work to identify what a person's tastes in pornography reveal about the nature of their desires, attitudes, and other attendant sins entangled with lust. All pornography is sinful and there is no such thing as "safe porn," but particular interests and curiosities may require more intense counsel or even therapy or incarceration (see below). In general, the more violent or "extreme" a person's tastes, the more pastoral counsel will need to address underlying issues of anger, control, perhaps past or present abuse perpetrated against or *by* the porn user. Porn that involves extreme sexual perversions like rape, incest, or bestiality are not likely to be handled by routine pastoral counseling alone.

4. Discipline

Discipline is not simply punitive but preemptive. It is first and foremost training. Therefore, a pastor must lead the way in demystifying pornography as an issue before his congregation or in men's and women's ministry environments. Beyond that, however, in personal cases, there may be cause for formal discipline.

If a person is involved with child pornography or other extreme or criminal perversions, the proper legal authorities should also be notified. Those cases are not simply a spiritual or ecclesial matter but also a criminal one. In other cases of porn use deemed serious enough, the formal process of church discipline may be in order, but this should not be the first resort. Formal discipline over using pornography may only be employed as the final resort in the case of ongoing porn use for which a member is unrepentant and unwilling to address. If the person is *struggling* with the sin, that is in itself a good sign.

5. Pointing to the Gospel

Your chief role as spiritual shepherd is to point sinners to the gospel, which announces the only freedom from sin, the only power to resist temptation and obey, and the only hope for joy that dispossesses us of the temporary, fleeting, sinful pleasures of the world. So as a pastor, you must make sure to lead your church well: Are your service's songs gospel-rich? Do they exalt the glory of Christ? Do your sermons center on the finished work of Christ? Do their exhortations to obedience flow from the justification found by grace through faith? Do your counselors work from a gospel-centered position? Are you cultivating a culture of grace in your church or a culture of law?

The Community's Role

Every sin is fundamentally a worship problem, and this is certainly true of the sin of pornography. Therefore, it is simply not enough for the local church to acknowledge that porn is wrong. That's the minimum information about porn, but it's not the only information. How a church works out her understanding of grace for sin and her understanding of sin itself will direct how it treats sinners dealing with porn. Here are a few important components of the church's application of "gospel training" in relation to pornography:

1. Accountability

Accountability is always good, but two general rules of thumb for how it ought to be structured are these: 1) A porn user should not have as his or her accountability partner another person who struggles with porn. The partner should be someone (of the same sex) who has either lived in extended victory over this sin or never seriously fallen prey to it. 2) The accountability partner should be someone who understands the gospel well and can point their partner to it time and again in non-flippant, direct, sincere ways. Think of Paul in Galatians 2 confronting Peter about his conduct not being in step with the truth of the gospel. In addition, the accountability should actually be accountability. There needs to be some "teeth" implied to someone's failure to fight or refusal to repent—not simply a rehearsal of the commandments not to lust, but the possibility of discipline.

2. Encouragement

The body of Christ is meant to be both a proclaimer and an adorner of the gospel. As Ray Ortlund says, we do not simply need gospel truth—though that's non-negotiable!—but also *a gospel culture.* The church that is over time pointing each other to the gospel of Jesus should over time see the gospel coming more and more to bear in the life of the community. Grace begets grace. And a church environment that labors faithfully not to simply preach the gospel, but to adorn the gospel with a gracious climate will become an unsafe place for sin, yet a safe place for sinners. Watch people grow in boldness to confess and repent, because they realize in this glorious light of transparency and humility and mercy that their sin shrinks into nothingness. In this same light, sinners find the impulse to repent more natural and find their own sense of identity in Christ more immediate.

3. Discipleship

A church committed to helping her people fight sin will have reliable discipleship structures in place, in which more mature believers are replicating themselves by befriending, teaching, counseling, and helping (in a thousand other ways) newer or less mature believers follow Jesus. If your church does not have a dedicated process to develop and reproduce disciples, you are not effectively helping your people fight sin (of any kind). You can preach about it until you're blue in the face, and it may have some immediate effect. But it's only in the community life of discipleship that we learn the applied wisdom of the gospel to trust that Jesus is better than what porn promises and train to fight our lustful appetites.

Discussion Questions

1. What would you say is our general disposition to the porn problem? Is it seen as the unforgivable sin? Is it seen as only the sin of the grossest kind of perverts?

2. If someone struggling with pornography was interested in confessing their sin to church leaders or a trusted partner, how confident should they be that they would not receive words of condemnation?

3. How is pornography a "worship problem"? What, in addition to sex, is being worshipped? What about other appetite sins like greed or gluttony? What is being worshipped besides money and food in these sins?

4. What are some ways you can work to demystify the issue of pornography?

What Does the Culture Say?

Matthew Lee Anderson

"MY FATHER OFTEN TOLD ME THAT IF NOT FOR PORNOGRA-phy, he'd have become a serial killer," Chris Offutt once wrote in the *New York Times*. On Offutt's telling, his father was both an avid consumer and creator of the dark medium, who made his living as one of America's most prolific pornographic novelists in the 1970s. But he also secretly drew a series of pornographic comics, which Offutt rather dispassionately reports "eventually ran 120 separate books, totaling 4,000 pages, depicting the torture of women."[13] Offutt rejects the story his father tried to sell him: "The idea that porn prevented him from killing women," he muses, "was a self-serving delusion that justified his impulse to write and draw portrayals of torture."[14] No, his father needed porn to save him because he couldn't come to grips with the simple fact that he *liked* it.

Theorists and sociologists have tussled for the past thirty years over whether pornography's easy availability makes violence more or less likely. The more pressing question, however, is why anyone became interested in the link in the first place. There is no need to take a stand on whether Offutt's father was right about the powers of pornography to save him from a murderous path. That he felt some deep connection between pornography and murder, between the depiction of women in graphic sexual poses and the violent destruction of their bodies should be enough to disturb us. Illicit sex and actual violence may be more closely connected than we might like to think.

Pornography deceives. Its sexualized depiction of human persons promises the viewer what it cannot deliver. But *how* pornography lies is difficult to see, if only because our eyes have gone blind from our frequent exposure to the medium. Pervasive consumption of pornography dulls the mind: if we delightedly give ourselves over to falsehoods, we lose our ability to sort truth from fiction. Sin has a compounding effect. The twin wraiths of confusion and ignorance preserve the charm of its false pleasures. It is easier for those drowning in a whirlpool of deceits to embrace their situation as "normal" than it is to escape.

The inescapable availability of pornography and the corrosive "pornification" of all other forms of media mean that the most pressing challenge for Christians is rediscovering what purity *feels* like. C. S. Lewis famously proposed that spiritual mediocrity is the equivalent of playing with mud pies instead of taking the holiday by the sea God offers us. Our situation is more dire, though: we are in danger of forgetting what the sea even offers. The warmth of sunshine that lifts our eyes and our hearts to heaven has been hidden by the stale pollution of our passions. Pornography is the only atmosphere we know. It has clotted our lungs, and we cannot get enough of it.

We have been told to accept porn as the new normal—which is perhaps the most pernicious and effective lie of all. Chris Offutt suggests that his father's secrecy was "born of shame and guilt." He does not moralize the tale. But he subtly implies that the source of his father's attraction to violent images is the stigma attached to his "mainstream" pornographic work. Had he simply accepted that we (and he) liked pornography—that pornography is normal—all might have been well. The thought is common enough in our culture, at least, even if Offutt does not agree with it. In fact, we have pressed the bounds of sexuality so far that "sex negativity" is our only sin left: any attempt to find a moral basis for sexuality *beyond* pleasure and consent is simply too prudish, too retrograde to be taken seriously in our enlightened age. Pornography is inescapable; therefore, it must be permissible. There is no other way for us, much less a "more excellent" one.

Imagining a world that has not so cheapened human sexuality, then, is the first act of resistance to the many lies pornography tells. A porn-saturated world or life is not *inevitable*; there is nothing in the cosmos that says it must be a permanent feature of our experience. To confess this, and to acknowledge our own responsibility in making the world we have, is to take the first steps toward freedom. By the grace of God, we can live in a world other than that which we now know. That such a thought is so foreign to most of our society betrays how *weak* the pornography-regime is. The moment we begin contemplating the prospect of living otherwise, the whole shoddy artifice that makes it seem attractive collapses into rubble. Finding a "more excellent way" begins with remembering that another way is possible, which is a thought that the pornography industry does not want anyone to truly believe.

Why might a deep and compulsive habit of creating violent pornography prevent a man from becoming a murderer? Pornography may represent a less vicious deviance than that which murder depends upon, but it trades on the same destructive, dehumanizing impulses. And comparing the two disturbs our complacent, lazy acceptance of pornography as a benign and harmless form of amusement. It shocks us because the widespread use of pornography seems so natural, so inevitable. It horrifies us because the world of pornography is our world. It cannot be, it *must* not be true. But it is.

The Death of Wonder and the Trivialization of What Matters

"Let wonder seem familiar," Shakespeare has written, "and to the chapel let us presently." The line is from his play *Much Ado about Nothing,* which is nothing if not a wondrous tale. A young man mistakenly accuses his fiancé of infidelity, and she faints upon the unjust slander. He believes her dead, and sorrowfully repents upon learning his error. All is made well at a wedding, where he is stunned by the vision of his fiancé alive and chastened by her offering of forgiveness. The friar is the one who instructs us all to become friends with wonder, provided that we make our way off to the chapel for its formalization in due order. The advice is worth following.

The path toward seeing how pornography dehumanizes begins here, in thinking about the death of wonder in our hearts and our lives. But I do not speak of wonder about *sex*—not yet, anyway. The death of mystery in that realm is only one manifestation of a more general disease, a *pornification* of our eyes and our minds that extends well beyond the realm of sexual stimulation. Whether pornography is to blame for this more general problem, or vice versa, may remain subject to debate. My only interest is in arguing that what happens in pornography is not limited to sex.

Consider, for a moment, our practices of reading or watching other entertaining or informational "content." Our minds are often hurried and frantic, which keeps our attention strictly on the surface of things. Any pleasures that come from reading must be had quickly (especially when reading online), or we give up on the task. We skim articles and book chapters, hastily moving on to consume the next bit of information. Our eyes jump from photo to photo while scrolling our phones in line at the store. We flit about from channel to channel, awaiting the next spectacle that can seize our attention. Ours is a life in *the shallows,* to use Nicholar Carr's fine phrase.[15] We rarely expend the effort required to contemplate any further than what appears in our direct line of sight, gorging ourselves on surfaces and images until we finally grow weary and eventually fall asleep.

This ravenous lust of vision is classically known as *curiositas,* curiosity.[16] *Curiositas* is a restlessness of the spirit and mind, an unsettled anxiety that pursues new spectacles to consume. Such pleasurable novelties provide cheap mental stimulation with little to no work.

The momentary Facebook check "just to see" gives us a brief respite from the responsibilities before us. We may not care about what we find; what matters is that we have found something new and that we are entertained. Curiosity fixes our attention on the "things below," the things that are seen, the things that we can dispense with the moment we are done. But because such visions lack depth they will never satisfy. And because they are ubiquitous they must become more outlandish. The only way to arrest the attention of the curious is by making a scene, and then attempting to outdo yourself the next time around.

A society animated by curiosity will have two compatible, paradoxical sentiments. First, it will attempt to peel back the curtain and lay bare sordid and dirty secrets. Curiosity aims to expose what ought not be known. Our society's rampant fascination with the inner workings of the lives of celebrities—lives we will never have—may seem benign. But the voyeurism that moves someone to gaze lustfully through a window operates according to the same logic, only in a sexual key. We will have our spectacles wherever we can find them—and the more secret they are, the better for us. Second, curiosity undercuts our stomach for more serious ventures. "Cat videos don't *really* matter," we say—and that is why our interest in them is damning. Curiosity is attentive only to the surface. It cannot abide the *matter*, the *substance*, or the *depths* before us. Curiosity is content with the image; but loving attention needs bodies. The curious has not the patience required for sustained consideration, much less the openness to the consuming immersiveness of wondrous rapture.

It is easy to see the spirit of *curiositas* at work in pornography. Porn offers the most alluring sort of spectacle. Depictions of individuals engaged in secret acts of grave importance can be viewed, enjoyed, and discarded with no investment or pain on the part of the viewer. The rapid-fire, disposable quality of pornography suits and fosters the restlessness of those who view it. It leads them to continue scrolling and hunting for the look or scene that might momentarily awaken their imaginations. All that matters are the surfaces, and the more and more provocative, the better.

There is no room within *curiositas* for reverential awe, for a sense that there are some mysteries that are not ours to unveil. The Christian objection to porn is not motivated by a fear of sexuality or by "sex negativity," but by a sanctified sense of wonder at the beauty of the human being, fully alive and fully revealed. And such wondrous treasures *want* secrecy; hiddenness is the native habitat of glory. But our curious society has long shed its reluctance to profane the most holy places. The body in its sexual presentation is now merely one more trivial amusement meant for the satisfaction of momentary and passing interests, leaving no permanent mark on the soul or the society. Sex no longer matters—which is why it will no longer be fun. For the comedy, the ordinariness, and the mundane weirdness of sex draw energy and life from the enchanted awe that tempts us to kneel in chaste humility before the glory of another human being. No longer sacred, sex has become nothing at all.

Obscenities and the Modesty of Desire

Reflect for a moment upon an obscenity. We know the options well enough. Such words have power because they violently expose what is normally hidden. Ephesians 5:12 suggests that it is "shameful even to mention what is done by them in secret." The obscenity takes such matters and *makes a scene* of them, forcing our mind's eye into the darkness of holy places. When reverence dies, such words lose their force. Our culture's widespread acceptance of certain words can be explained this way.

The restriction of Ephesians 5:12, though, poses a problem for writing about pornography, a problem that also helps explain how pornography lies. As Christians, we are tasked with critiquing pornography without awakening illicit desires ourselves. If we are too explicit, we engage in the kind of *obscenities* we are denouncing—a problem shock-jock pastors have sometimes fallen into.

Strategic ambiguity about matters of sexuality is essential for protecting love.[17] Those in love are sometimes so swept up in their games that they do not realize the passions forming beneath them. But once love arises, it delights in preserving a hidden core known by the couple alone. The first time couples tell their engagement stories serves well as a paradigmatic example of this. There is often a gap in the tale somewhere after she says "yes" which is frequently filled by the highly suggestive "and then we said some stuff." They mean, of course, that they kissed madly and furiously. And appropriately so. But lovers delight in speaking elusively about their most intimate expressions. Naming them directly spoils a good deal of the fun. Song of Solomon is an erotically charged book precisely because it is *not* a sex manual; it hides the physical intimacy where it belongs, behind the veil of metaphors, allusions, and analogies.[18]

Pornography betrays love's natural inclination toward privacy. But in doing so, it can only depict distortions of the real thing to us. Pornography is an exemplary instance of the "observer's paradox," which says that the subject under observation is unwittingly influenced by the presence of a third party. The observer's paradox means that publicity changes the event; performing before an audience is a different kind of act than practicing in private. Love's true character can be known only by those experiencing it first-hand. Viewing an act of love from the outside does not allow us to see what we think we are viewing. If love is really present, it can only be felt and known within the faces and bodies of those engaging in it. Pornographers understand this, which is why virtual-reality porn and sex-bots are in our society's (near) future. They promise to simulate the face-to-face character of sexual desire better than a computer screen can.

And we can go further down this path. What happens within an unobserved room is necessarily different for the couple itself when a camera is present. The face-to-face character of desire is not meant to be *displayed,* but enjoyed. Lovers who record their own sexual activity for their own private enjoyment later allow the structure and logic of pornography to determine their own union—even if they are married. And they do not record their own love, but a subtly distorted imitation of it, as they introduce a willingness on their part to be viewed from the outside—even if they are the only ones watching. Such mimicry may appear, on the surface, to be the pure display of marital intimacy. But when we go beneath the surface it becomes clear that marital unions can surrender to the pornographic, even if they do not produce or watch commercially produced pornography.

Pornography lies, then, by imitating the pleasures and the sacrifices of love, and destroys them in the process. But death can mimic life persuasively for only so long. We are hurtling fast toward pornography's triumphal destruction of the romance that once guarded and preserved our relationships. By turning the central mystery of human sexuality into a public display, pornography undermines the rules and conventions that both honored sex and made sin possible. When sexual pleasure assumed the throne of our hearts, romance was the inevitable victim. Romance and marriage are too much work when sex and pornography are a swipe or click away. Hollywood's happy endings may have made us believe too easily that marriage is effortless and simple—but they were also one of our last bulwarks against the banal degradation of sex. The pornified mind cannot be bothered with the adornment of foreplay, much less the patient and constant pursuit of one's spouse. Though such burdens give the act more meaning and significance, they take time and energy to happily sustain. Why bother as long as the easy pleasures of porn are at hand?

Objectification and Porn

Industrialized sex profits off of orgasms, which means that they need to be had on the cheap. And so the industry manufactures pleasures with as few costs to the producer or consumer as possible. Time is money: Offutt's dad "wrote" his "novels" in as few as three days. And labor is plentiful. Women in porn are shockingly dispensable; they have "shelf lives" of only a few short years, if they survive past first exposure at all.[19] And real women will soon be irrelevant to the process, anyway. Digitally created, CGI porn will be cheap and easy to produce, making "victimless" porn a real possibility.[20]

But it is the orgasms of the audience that make pornographers money, not those of the performers. The man who watches pornography is *himself* the product; it is his pleasure that the industry aims at, his satisfaction that matters most of all. The women and men who perform before an audience become objects of their audience's gratification. But the bitter, brutal irony of the pornography industry is that by aiming at such pleasure the audience objectifies *itself* by becoming a product in a commercial transaction. Porn degrades everyone involved in it, but its customers most of all—for they are the unwitting dupes who do not realize the game that is being played against them.

Where is the viewer of pornography when they watch a scene, and why does it arouse them? In its central case, sexual desire aims at reciprocity. Arousal happens when we are drawn not simply to a beautiful person, but when we notice that person welcoming and returning our interest. We want to be wanted, and sexual desire is our bodily recognition that we are desired in a similar, bodily way. Pornography trades on the hope that we will be desired. We believe that the woman looking back at us wants us, that she is "ours" in the way a spouse might one day become.

The viewer of pornography, then, places themselves imaginatively *within* the scene.[21] There is a kind of "empathy" at work in such viewership, a self-identification that happens between ourselves and the subjects being depicted. The audience at *King Lear* feels all of his sorrow by seeing themselves manifested in Lear's mistakes, and his own decline as illuminating their own challenges. But this empathetic identification means that viewing is never neutral; watching entangles our wills by presenting us with a point of view and requiring that we accept or reject it. If we delight when characters in novels do wrong—we are really doing something wrong. The self-identification between the viewer and the subject is what makes pornography attractive, and what makes it bad. Imagining ourselves in such scenarios is a morally potent act, in that our wills affirm the acts as they are happening.

Pornography, if it is anything, cannot be morally trivial. But this identification of the self with what we are viewing betrays the expansive and unrestrained narcissistic greed at the heart of the pornographic world. The women who look out from the screen do not merely want *us,* but our most fantastic and delusional portraits of our selves. In order for the fiction that they desire us to have any sense, we must (momentarily, at least) think ourselves desirable. Such an irrational, unfounded wishfulness only survives by feeding itself on more lies—so the depiction of one woman goes up to two, and so the harem is born. Beneath pornography is the supposition that the mere fact of our desire for a woman makes us worthy of her; and, so, not being bound by any kind of norm, desire must proceed endlessly. It is no surprise that the industrialized, cheap and easy sex of pornography has answered and evoked an almost unrestrained sexual greed, which allows us to be gods and goddesses within the safety of our own fantasies. It is for deep and important reasons that the Ten Commandments use the economic language of "coveting" to describe the badness of errant sexual desires.

The empathetic imagining of themselves in a pornography scene, though, does turn the other participants into objects and instruments for our own satisfaction. What are all the other characters in the scene *for*? Nothing, save our own self-indulgence. Pornography reduces conversation and relationship from an intimate disclosure of our personhood to an irritating way station on the quick path to sexual pleasure. Elaborate and sophisticated stories function as little more than extended fore-play for the pornographic.[22] And all the participants disappear when our payoff arrives. We click to a new page, we turn off the sex-bot so we can go get lunch, we furtively flee the prostitute and return to our "real" lives. The scenarios are different. The logic is the same. In each case, the woman is nothing more than an instrument to our own fantastical pleasures; she is a tool that we discard the moment we find a more satisfactory widget. The people of pornography are no more irreplaceable than salad forks. If one gets tired or boring, swap it for another and no harm is (ostensibly) done.

Pornography is not bad because it causes adultery.[23] Instead, it is bad because the user acts *as if* committing adultery. Pornography is stimulating because we affirmatively imagine ourselves in sexual acts not involving our spouses. Pornography use means one's spouse is fungible or replaceable with respect to sexual activity, an activity that is central to the shape and mean-ing of marriage. And this is so even if we do not realize that is what we are doing. It is possible to do great wrongs without knowing, or even intending them. Marriage is a union of only two, and no others. Pornography replaces one member, reducing them from an equal partner to an instrument for personal gratification.

The Peopling of the World

Pornography is a murder of the heart. Is this too strong? Or must we use such language to wake us from the slumbering injustice in which we live?

Perhaps, if our eyes were able to break through the smoggy haze of our pornified society, we would see the slow, steady hand of death at work all around us. Perhaps we would awake into the terror that those who once knew of holiness felt. Perhaps if we would recognize the desecration of the temple of the living God that we are all, every day, complicit in, we would pray to the same Lord for mercy.

Reducing the human person to an instrument for our own pleasure is to wish in our hearts that they simply did not exist as persons. If we believe human beings can be replaced by sex-bots or virtual-reality pornography, what good are they, precisely? Persons are independent centers of agency, with their own wills and minds and reason. They cannot be traded, like baseball cards, on the basis that one brings us more sexual pleasure than another. To do so violates the very nature of their humanity. Pornography, I say again, is a form of murder within the heart.

Which is why, eventually, pornography obscures or violates the faces of the women who are drawn into it. From the eyes and the mouth flow forth speech and song and poetry and all the marks that make humans mysteries. But as pornography progresses, the person is—*effaced*. The locus of their personal presence is reduced to a receptacle of our own projective fantasies. "In pornography the face has no role to play," Roger Scruton has written, "other than to be subjected to the empire of the body."[24]

Against such violence we can only respond as Shakespeare did: "The world must be peopled!" Pornography *de*peoples the world. I have mentioned that it hangs on the pretense that the human beings around us are instruments for our pleasure. But making people tools allows us to pretend that we have no obligations toward them, that they cannot make a claim on us. There is no sharper contrast with such a life than babies, who show a delightfully flagrant disregard for the pleasures of their parents. Parents love their little humans in part because they are tiny, adorable bundles of obligations. A sexuality ordered appropriately will bear fruit—in children, yes, but also in being empowered by the Spirit to joyfully welcome the other human bundles of needs into our lives, even if we are not ourselves married. The world must be peopled—we must be people within the world, serving one another. Pornography stands in the way of this.

"Let wonder seem familiar, and to the chapel let us presently." For confession and repentance, for renewal and forgiveness, for the manner of our treatment of one another, a manner that we are *all* participants in—and for, above all, the hope of the gospel. We are restored as people in the word of grace, set free from the bondage of "inevitability" for our sins. At the cross of Christ, every human life finds a worth that is inestimable. Christ has died for all! How shall we not meet each other with a chaste and holy reverence, with a sanctified fear and trembling that is a mark of our salvation? The lives of those who make and consume pornography bear the stamp, the *image* of Jesus Christ. When we finally see them as they are, with the clear eyes of purity, we will know either awe for their majesty or sorrow for its marring. Let such wonder be familiar; within it lies the wellspring of hope.

Discussion Questions

1. What is your earliest memory of understanding what pornography is and how our society has been influenced by porn? How do you feel it may have influenced your feelings and knowledge of sexuality and intimacy since?

2. "When sexual pleasure assumed the throne of our hearts, romance was the inevitable victim." Do you agree or disagree with this statement? If true, how might this affect singleness and dating relationships within the church community? How might it affect marriages?

3. How has the pornification of our culture distorted our view of other people?

ADDITIONAL READING

Undefiled by Harry Schaumburg

Purity Is Possible by Helen Thorne

Not Even a Hint by Joshua Harris

Finally Free: Fighting for Purity with the Power of Grace by Heath Lambert

Wired for Intimacy: How Pornography Hijacks the Male Brain by William M. Struthers

ACKNOWLEDGMENTS

TO THE MANY HANDS INSIDE AND OUTSIDE THE ERLC, WE thank you for your help and assistance on this book. The ERLC team provided joyful encouragement in the planning and execution of this series, and without them, it would never have gotten off the ground. We want to also personally thank Phillip Bethancourt who was a major visionary behind this project. We'd also like to thank Jennifer Lyell and Devin Maddox at B&H, our publisher, for their work in guiding us through this process.

ABOUT THE ERLC

THE ERLC IS DEDICATED TO ENGAGING THE CULTURE WITH the gospel of Jesus Christ and speaking to issues in the public square for the protection of religious liberty and human flourishing. Our vision can be summed up in three words: kingdom, culture, and mission. Since its inception, the ERLC has been defined around a holistic vision of the kingdom of God, leading the culture to change within the church itself and then as the church addresses the world. The ERLC has offices in Washington, DC, and Nashville, Tennessee.

ABOUT THE CONTRIBUTORS

Matthew Lee Anderson is the founder and lead writer at Mere Orthodoxy. He is the author of *Earthen Vessels: Why Our Bodies Matter to Our Faith* and *The End of Our Exploring: A Book about Questioning and the Confidence of Faith*. Anderson is also a perpetual member of Biola University's Torrey Honors Institute.

Russell Moore is president of the ERLC. In this role, he leads the organization in all its efforts to connect the agenda of the kingdom of Christ to the cultures of local congregations for the sake of the mission of the gospel in the world. He holds a PhD in systematic theology from The Southern Baptist Theological Seminary. He is the author of several books, including *Onward: Engaging the Culture without Losing the Gospel*. He and his wife, Maria, are the parents of five boys.

Courtney Reissig is a wife, mom, and writer. She is the author of *The Accidental Feminist: Restoring Our Delight in God's Good Design*. She lives with her family in Little Rock, Arkansas.

Trevin Wax is Bible and Reference Publisher for LifeWay Christian Resources. He is the author of multiple books, including *Gospel-Centered Teaching, Clear Winter Nights,* and *Counterfeit Gospels*. He blogs regularly at Kingdom People, hosted by The Gospel Coalition. He and his wife, Corina, have three children.

Jared C. Wilson is director of content strategy for Midwestern Seminary, managing editor of For The Church (ftc.com), and author of several books, including *Gospel Wakefulness, The Story of Everything,* and *Unparalleled*. He lives near Kansas City, Missouri, with his wife, Becky, and their two daughters.

NOTES

1. Jonathan Grant, *Divine Sex* (Grand Rapids, MI: Brazos Press, 2015), 121.

2. *The Collected Works of G. K. Chesterton*, Volume 21: *The Illustrated London News, 1932–34* (San Francisco, CA: Ignatius Press, 2011), 391.

3. Scot McKnight, *One Life: Jesus Calls, We Follow* (Grand Rapids, MI: Zondervan, 2010), 109.

4. Frederick Buechner, *A Room Called Remember: Uncollected Pieces* (San Francisco, CA: Harper and Row, 1984), 18.

5. I elaborate on practical steps to overcoming temptation in *Tempted and Tried: Temptation and the Triumph of Christ* (Wheaton, IL: Crossway, 2011).

6. Buechner, *A Room Called Remember*, 18.

7. See http://jonathanmerritt.religionnews.com/2016/01/20/christians-pornography-problem/.

8. As quoted in Carolyn McCulley's *Radical Womanhood* (Chicago, IL: Moody Press, 2008), 166–67.

9. Ariel Levy, *Female Chauvinist Pigs: Women and the Rise of Raunch Culture* (New York, NY: Simon & Schuster, 2005), 35.

10. See http://www.thisamericanlife.org/radio-archives/episode/557/transcript.

11. All personal stories shared in this chapter are true but the names have been changed.

12. Thomas Chalmers, "The Expulsive Power of a New Affection" in *The Works of Thomas Chalmers* (Philadelphia, PA: A. Towar, Hogan & Thompson, 1833), 381–82.

13. Chris Offutt, "My Dad the Pornographer," *New York Times*, February 15, 2015. Available at http://www.nytimes.com/2015/02/08/magazine/my-dad-the-pornographer.html. Accessed March 16, 2016.

14. Ibid.

15. See Nicholas Carr, *The Shallows: What the Internet Is Doing to Our Brains* (New York, NY: W. W. Norton, 2011).

16. My favorite treatment of the subject is Paul Griffiths's *Intellectual Appetite: A Theological Grammar* (Washington, DC: CUA Press, 2009).

17. Paul's commendation of verbal modesty in Ephesians 5 suggests he understands this.

18. And lest we think verbal modesty cannot be any fun, we should also observe that it is precisely what keeps sexual humor alive: a sly double-entendre that only one's spouse understands is only an amusement if such acts are never named directly.

19. Men who "succeed" tend to have longer careers. The difference is worth considering.

20. And if not that, sex-bots will serve the same function pornography does now. This is the only *very small* benefit to computers taking over everyone's jobs.

21. The person who views pornography for non-erotic purposes, of course, does not—though the possibility of being entangled within its snares is always a live one.

22. One way to distinguish whether an image of sexuality is "pornographic" or not is to determine what it serves: Does something essential happen within it that enhances and deepens the story? Or is it merely gratuitous?

23. If there is a causal link between pornography use and adultery, it is only in the aggregate. Many men and women who use pornography

never commit adultery. But the badness of such an action is not dependent upon the "consequences" alone.

23. Roger Scruton, *The Face of God* (London, UK: Bloomsbury Publishing, 2012), 107.

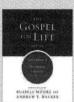
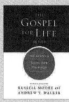

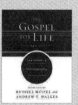
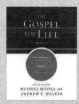